Charles Way

Charles Way has written over fifty plays and specialises in writing for children, young people and family audiences. His plays are performed worldwide. Charles has won several major awards – *A Spell of Cold Weather* won a Writer's Guild award in 2001, in 2004 he received the English Arts Council award for *Red Red Shoes* and in 2010 he won the German Children's theatre prize for *Missing*. Charles is also well known for his versions of classic tales such as Sleeping Beauty, Cinderella and The Snow Queen. He has also written many plays for radio, and a TV poem for BBC 2, *No Borders*, set on the Welsh borders, where he lives and has spent most of his creative life.

www.charles-way.co.uk

First published in the UK in 2013 by Aurora Metro Publications Ltd

67 Grove Avenue, Twickenham, TW1 4HX

www.aurorametro.com info@aurorametro.com

Missing © 2013 Charles Way

Pirates! © 2013 Charles Way

Nivelli's War © 2013 Charles Way

Production: Simon Smith

With thanks to: Martin Gilbert, Neil Gregory, Richard Turk, Jack Timney, Juliet Peacock, Anna Festa, Fay Allum, Alex Chambers

10 9 8 7 6 5 4 3 2 1

Printed by imprintdigital.com, Exeter, UK

ISBN: 978-1-906582-51-7

CONTENTS

Foreword

Children's and young people's theatre is developing across the world and ideas about theatre and children's relationship to it vary from country to country. The three plays in this volume were commissioned by companies in four different countries: England, Northern Ireland, Germany and America, and as a result the plays reflect the artistic practice of these countries and the different expectations of what 'children's theatre' should be trying to achieve. The plays could not be more different from each other, but what they have in common is a desire to explore the lives and experiences of children in the world today – in ways that are exciting, fun and truthful. The plays were all written for professional companies but are equally valid in the context of young performers, in schools or youth theatres.

Over many years of experience I have found that it's almost impossible for a critic to see a good new play in a poor production. These plays were all blessed with excellent first productions and I would like to thank Andrea Kramer from Consol Theatre in Gelsenkirchen, Germany and Kevin Lewis of Theatr Iolo in Wales for their two very different takes on the same play *Missing*, which is an experiment in form and content and leaves much to the director's discretion. Watching the play in the German language was revealing in itself – as the text becomes a kind of music that sits above the action – and allowed me to see the structure of the piece in purely emotional terms. It is an upsetting piece – but not without hope.

Janet Stanford of Imagination Stage, USA and Jon Lloyd from the Polka theatre UK both produced versions of *Pirates!* that were fast and funny. The designs were imaginative and often spectacular as the play moves magically from a modern boy's bedroom to the deck of an 18th century pirate ship. It is fascinating to watch children watch this play – as its underlying themes became apparent to them – and they discover for themselves that this is more than a pirate play, it's a play about a kid dealing with his emotional life in respect to his parents' separation, and as this dawns upon them they become full and deep participants in the action.

Paul Boscoe McEneaney of Cahoots NI Children's Theatre in Belfast is a director whose first theatrical love was 'Magic'. He is a skilled conjuror himself and gave me a great gift when he asked me to find a story in which the art of the conjuror was fully embedded in the core of the action. It was by chance that I came upon Herbert Levin – a magician who in the 1930s wrote his name backwards – to become 'Nivelli' as a means of escaping the anti-Jewish sentiments that were sweeping across Germany. He became well-known under this name as a magician but it could not save him from Auschwitz. He did however survive the camp by teaching his Nazi guards how to perform tricks by sleight of hand. *Nivelli's War* is not an account of his life, but my story is inspired by his, and contains within it the reckless optimism contained in all magic – that sometimes the most intransigent things, situations and feelings can be changed, transformed, made new.

Charles Way

INTRODUCTION

The first thing that readers of Charles Way's plays will notice with this new collection is that the titles are not familiar. There are no Cinderellas or Sinbads in the line-up but instead three wholly original stories which, even when they involve historical settings, feel like they are ripped from yesterday's headlines. Way has said that he is essentially always writing about what 'bugs' him and it seems that what has been bugging him lately are issues like child neglect, abandonment, divorce, kidnapping and the terrible human costs of war. While Way's reputation for breathing contemporary life into classic fairytales is well-established, these three pieces all have a sense of urgency and immediacy about them which makes compelling and powerful theatre for today's audiences the world over.

MISSING

Written for two theatres located in German and Welsh mining towns, *Missing* is distantly inspired by the Grimm's fairy tale of Hansel and Gretel but more immediately by the question, "What does it mean nowadays to grow up poor in an economically depressed town?" Way tells the story from the viewpoints of all four characters – the Dad, the Stepmother, Hansel, a withdrawn and alienated teenager, and Grethel, his much younger sister who has a mental disability that leaves her vulnerable to bullies and evil-doers. When Hansel – like a detective – traces his sister's disappearance to the horrible truth, he is still hampered by cops who have him pegged as a juvenile delinquent and a father who is rarely sober enough to act. A tragic outcome seems all but certain until Hansel's daring plan to lure the kidnapper with a suitcase full of money pays off. As risky in form as it is in content, this piece leaves the assignment of specific lines to the discretion of each producing company and demands a creative use of movement to support and, in places, replace the text. Evocative and eloquent on the page, *Missing* has proven its effectiveness in production and in 2010 was honored with the highly prestigious German Children's Theatre Prize.

PIRATES!

Pirates! is also a bi-national co-commission which Way wrote for theaters in the London and the Washington, DC suburbs. The protagonist Jim is an eight year-old who is fascinated by 18th Century pirate lore. He is also on the brink of being reunited with the mother who left him and his father four years earlier for a life on the road with a new partner. As he struggles to come to terms with whether or not he wants to renew this relationship, Jim dreams that he is caught in an adventure on the high seas in which he must choose between allegiance to the charismatic female pirate Captain Freely or to her arch nemesis – the strict disciplinarian, Captain McGovern. Like most children touched by divorce, Jim's deepest wish is to force a stop to the fight between his parents. In a moment of striking theatrical imagery, Way has Jim interrupt the duel between the two warring captains and demand that they throw down their swords forever. Instead they pause just long enough to tell him,

"This is our fight lad – ours.

And you are not the cause of it.

'Tis time for you to go."

The fantastical journey into history allows Jim to process his fears about his very present dilemma. He gains the courage to speak directly to his father about the past and realizes that he can choose to what degree he wants to allow his mother back into his life. *Pirates!* was much praised by critics on both sides of the Atlantic for its premiere productions and was nominated for Washington's Helen Hayes Outstanding New Play Award in 2011 and given the Distinguished New Play Award by the American Alliance for Theatre and Education in 2012.

NIVELLI'S WAR

Written for Belfast based Cahoots, NI, *Nivelli's War* is set in Germany in the aftermath of World War II where displaced people are desperately trying to return home to find their loved ones. Six-year old Ernst is an evacuee who finds himself alone on his aunt's farm two hundred kilometers from Frankfurt am Main with only a mysterious chicken thief to turn to for help. The story of the unlikely bond between Mr. H (the thief) and Ernst and their difficult journey home is literally conjured up before our eyes by a world famous, yet strangely weary, magician – the Mr. Nivelli of the play's title. As he prepares on stage for the night's performance, he blows up a balloon that transports us back through time to key moments in the past that still tug at his mind: the parting with his mother after a devastating bombing of the city; his aunt Sophie wandering off insane with grief; the cart Mr. H makes from his uncle's bicycle in order to carry the boy along the road; the Russian soldiers Mr. H distracts with sleight-of-hand tricks; and an aristocrat and her butler hiding out in a boarded-up mansion who offer the travelers a rare evening of respite – a warm fire and a decent meal. The acclaimed magician has devoted his life to the art that his friend and savior taught him, a friend who he learns was a Jew and whose survival in Nazi Germany seems to have been for the sole purpose of delivering little Ernst back into his mother's arms. How to repay such a debt? Can Ernst or any of us, trapped in the inhumanity of war, ever become whole again?

Despite the big questions and dark themes that Charles Way explores in these plays, what shines through as ever in his writing is a generous and complex understanding of human nature. Many of the adult characters seem lost, barely able to direct themselves let alone their children. They may be beaten down by life, emotionally stifled, self-involved, alcoholic or even insane but the playwright always reveals their essence. Even the would-be murderess in *Missing* discloses a history of neglect which allows us, if not to forgive her, then at least to accept why she has become the way she is. The three boy protagonists, therefore, who bravely navigate the worlds of these plays, face enormous odds. As they carve their own paths forward through their stories they must, at the same time, invent a moral compass to live by. Love and loyalty are abiding virtues that resonate for all. But answers are never obvious or attainable by logic. A thief turns out to be a savior. A shark proves sympathetic, sentimental even. And a drunk dad with a big lump of wood comes through just when you least expect it!

Way directs his audience to a sub-conscious space for answers of a deeply personal nature to the issues of our time. Through nightmares, dreams and memories, in passages of movement that echo or replace the text, he leads us beyond intellect in these plays. He imprints images in our minds – a brother and sister burning a garbage bag full of money; a boy caught between two swords trying to end an eternal duel; a magician floating upward under a bunch of balloons – images that defy literal explanation but that communicate directly from the stage to the soul.

Janet Stanford

Artistic Director, Imagination Stage, Bethesda, MD, USA

MISSING

Missing, or 'Looking for Grethel' was jointly commissioned by Consol Theatre, Gelsenkirchen, Germany and Theatr Iolo, Cardiff, Wales. For ages 10 and over.

Characters	Welsh	German
Hansel	Nick Hywell	Tobias Novo
Grethel	Lucy Rivers	Hanna Charlotte Kruger
Father	John Norton	Markus Kirschbaum.
Stepmother	Caroline Bunce	Eva Horstmann

Cousin of Stepmother *(Played by Father)*

The play was written for a cast of four – two male and two female.

Part 1: Hansel and his Family

Part 2: Looking Back – Four Points of View

Part 3: Looking for Grethel

Part 4: Aftermath – Four Points of View

Notes

Missing is a piece of physical theatre with text. There are occasions when movement/action alone will be all that is needed to tell the story, and the text is an active 'stage direction'. To indicate this I have underlined certain sections which are quite clearly not necessary as spoken text. These are examples only and the director/company may make other choices depending on the nature of the production.

The opening prologue is shared by all the cast, and the following sections are led by one character, as indicated by the larger numbered headings. However, these are not required to be monologues. Within each section I have indicated which lines would belong to characters other than the lead.

PART ONE

Hansel and his Family

1 CAST

The papers said he looked like something the devil cooked up for dinner

They didn't like the way he hid his face with a hood

They didn't like the way he clung to the shadows

To the side of the street – like a cat – up to no good.

His name is Hansel.

From his bedroom window Hansel can see the old mine

Where his grandfather used to work.

It's a huge, red rotting thing

An iron shape cut out against a clear sky.

Sometimes Hansel climbs up the side of the air shaft through rusting iron hoops

On to a ledge that gives a good view of the field, the mine and the city beyond.

It's forbidden of course but he likes it there – he sits and smokes – watching the city lights –

Up there no one can creep up from behind

It feels safe and gives him a chance to think.

What does Hansel think about?

His family.

His father – used to work the mine too before it closed down.

After that he became a driver delivering parcels all over Europe.

Until he lost the job.

He says he misses his friends from the old days and that's why he drinks.

He says work gave his drinking shape – but now he can drink all day.

On those days he forgets to ask Hansel –

Where have you been?

Who were you with?

What were you doing?

Come home at a reasonable time.

The only thing Hansel does is look after his little sister –

Grethel.

His mother had asked him to do this – she trusted him –

And he does – he looks after her – protects her.

Sometimes he fights for her – with his bare fists in the field below.

Where's their mother?

She's dead.

She died when Hansel was ten.

When he was twelve his father married again.

Once he told Hansel that he loved alcohol more than he loved his new wife –

Their stepmother.

At first Grethel was pleased – she so wanted a mother – like the one Hansel spoke about –

A mother who loved you – who told you stories.

PART TWO

Looking Back – Four Points of View

1 HANSEL

Grethel was very young when mother died.

When Father told her she was going to have a new Mum, Grethel was happy. She smiled and smiled.

When stepmother didn't turn out to be what she'd imagined Grethel smiled even more –

Like she was too scared to relax her cheeks.

I didn't like our new mother from the start.

She was all smiles herself to begin with

But when she wasn't looking at us directly the smile dropped from her face

And her face was mean and hard.

At first the battle between us was silent.

She took over the house, which was what Father wanted.

She did everything for him, lots of little things he could easily have done for himself

Like collecting Grethel's child benefit money – or – paying the gas bill

And gradually he became – smaller and smaller – like he was shrinking.

He never asked me about anything – about why I didn't go to school or anything.

I tried to get work, but I'm not good with people.

To work in a cafe you have to smile and talk about things that don't mean anything.

I don't like talking – I feel weak after. Silence is powerful and I like that.

I did get a job once but I got the sack because I took money from the till.

Father said –

FATHER   You little thieving rat – you're no son of mine – You're a monster.

Which was good.

FATHER   I don't know where you bloody came from.

Which was odd.

His wife stood behind him smoking and smiling

STEPMOTHER   I told you so – I told you he was no good. The sooner he leaves this house the better.

They seemed to want me to respond – maybe give them a good reason to chuck me out –

But what about Grethel–?

I took the money to buy her some school stuff.

It's important that she keeps going to school –

And I don't want her to look out of place – or feel bad about having old things –

So I bought her a new plastic dinner box, and some cheese strings.

I can't leave her with them.

So I just stare at them – sullen, mean, angry

And in the end she gets scared –

STEPMOTHER Why are you staring at me – you little devil?

Result.

STEPMOTHER Stop staring.

But I don't stop. One night – the night – I go over to the mine.

I climb up through the hoops and sit on the ledge

The city is moving. Lights – travelling – here – there – where?

I hear police sirens and an ambulance.

I see the lights of the stadium and hear the crowd chanting.

Perhaps they'll get into the champion's league – but who cares – I don't.

In the field below I see a small figure walking. It looks like a girl. Grethel?

She's calling out, shouting something but she is too far away and the wind takes her voice.

Then I see another shape, moving slowly through the kids play area.

It waits there for a moment before moving forward – towards Grethel.

It's a man – I can tell that – even from here.

<u>I call out</u>

Grethel!

But she can't hear me either.

Perhaps it's a security guard – or someone she knows

Perhaps there's nothing to be scared of, or worried about – but I know there is.

I can tell by the way the man moves – looking around to see if anyone's watching.

I step back so my shape won't be seen against the sky.

I'm probably no more than a thousand yards away – but the wrong side of the perimeter fence

So I freeze – I watch.

She turns to see him and then she starts to walk away

Good girl – but then he must say something and she turns back.

They talk – then he gives her something – I can't tell what.

Then he turns and she follows him.

<u>I yell her name into the wind – I scream –</u>

GRETHEL!

But she doesn't look back – she takes his hand and they walk into the shadows. She takes his hand.

She's gone. Gone? No, no. It's eleven at night – Grethel's home asleep – where I left her. Why would she come out – this late? All I could see was a shape of a girl. It could have been anyone.

I climb down the ladder – almost fall – run home – and *she* is there.

<u>Not Grethel – Stepmother.</u>

STEPMOTHER   What you running from?

I run upstairs – open Grethel's door –

Grethel?

<u>She isn't there. I go down.</u>

Where's Grethel?

STEPMOTHER   What do you mean, 'Where's Grethel?'

She's not in her room.

<u>A silence.</u>

STEPMOTHER   Have you looked in the bathroom?

<u>I look in the bathroom</u> – it's empty. I go down.

She's not there – where is she?

STEPMOTHER   I don't know – why should I?

You were here.

STEPMOTHER   If you're worried go and look for her – you're her brother after all.

<u>I stare at her – she says</u>

STEPMOTHER   I can't go I've had a drink – nothing else to do.

She doesn't look drunk – or sound it.

STEPMOTHER   She's probably staying over with friends.

Who?

STEPMOTHER   How should I know? She'll phone in the morning.

I go back to Grethel's room – sit on the bed.

She's probably right. Grethel's with friends. It wasn't her at all.

I am tired – suddenly so tired –

I stare at the phone –

Perhaps I should call the police – but the police know me – what would they think? They wouldn't believe me – they'd laugh.

<u>I go back down.</u>

Where's Dad?

STEPMOTHER   Where do you think?

I walk to the club. He's not there. I ask around. He was there but he left.

I start to walk home taking the route he may have taken.

A police car passes – slows down. I stare at them and they drive off.

I see a figure in the street – lying down – as if asleep. He's drunk.

<u>I yell at him –</u>

Where's Grethel?

He starts to cry.

Then he covers his head as if I'm about to kick his head in.

Maybe I should – teach him a lesson. But I don't. I go home.

STEPMOTHER   Did you find him?

<u>I nod.</u>

Did she call?

STEPMOTHER   Who?

Did Grethel call?

STEPMOTHER   No – I found her phone.

I look at her phone. I check my own phone – dead – no credit – maybe she tried to call me.

STEPMOTHER   Where's your father?

On the pavement –

STEPMOTHER   He's a weak man – but don't you worry – I'll look after him. I'll look after all of us – even you.

I stare at her.

2 GRETHEL

I like to make things up. I don't mean lying – I just mean make things up. Like this teacher asked me what I'd had for breakfast – the real answer was – ice cream – because I'd found it in the fridge – but I said eggs and ham and fruit and cheese and bread and coffee –because that's what Jenny has in her house.

Sometimes I watch the TV for hours and afterwards I can't remember any of it.

I do that all the time – I like it – I drift off –

Though sometimes I get angry – really angry and once I ripped some curtains down at school and I got sent home. They said I'd sworn at a teacher – and I said sorry. I heard them say – it was 'typical' – I didn't know what that meant, 'typical'.

Most of the time I'm quiet. People ask me things and I don't hear them. I just hear their voices – a long way away and by the time I know they've been saying something to me – they've given up.

I always hear Hansel though.

I've got a new mother. She calls me 'Daddy's girl'.

My Dad says he loves me and he buys me big fluffy toys.

Once he bought me a big teddy bear – and it was bigger than me and when it caught fire – I burnt my hands and the fumes were so bad that Hansel had to carry me outside.

When I'm with Hansel I feel okay –

Hansel always defends me, and he got beaten up once in the big flat field by the big red mine. There's a playground there and it's got pretty coloured letters and stuff all over it – even on the rides. There's a plastic crocodile that moves up and down – and this big boy pushed me off and made me give him the money I'd been given to buy a kebab. I cried all the way home – but there was no one at home, except Hansel and he went and hit the boy in the mouth. A tooth came out – and I've still got it because it fell out right next to the crocodile.

A crocodile's tooth – that's what it is.

One night – the night –

I was upset because Dad wouldn't speak to me and I didn't know if I'd done something wrong. He wouldn't even look at me and I got scared. Stepmother told him to go for a drink. He looked sad and tired – like he wanted to cry. I don't like crying – when I asked stepmother what was wrong she said –

STEPMOTHER   Nothing.

And I knew that wasn't true.

<u>I asked</u>

Where's Hansel?

STEPMOTHER   I don't know – why don't you go and look for him?

I asked dad – is it alright to go looking for Hansel at eleven o'clock?

FATHER   Yes – go on – go and look for him –

And he looked away as if I wasn't there.

Stepmother said

STEPMOTHER   Go on then – but don't be long – I saw him in the park –

Near the crocodile?

STEPMOTHER   Yes.

She had a phone in her hand like she was waiting to call someone – and I went out looking for Hansel.

It was very windy – and dark too – but every now and then the moon came out – like it does in the stories Hansel tells me. He says our mother told him lots of stories.

I knew Hansel had a secret place but I didn't know where.

I thought he might see me – hear me – if I shouted loud enough.

HANSEL!

Then from the side of the park, where the crocodile is – I see a light – like a cigarette light and I think it's Hansel maybe – coming towards me – but it isn't –

It isn't Hansel.

3 FATHER

I'm often a little – under the influence – but that doesn't make what I say any the less true. People say things used to be better – in the old days – It wasn't. People were poor then in a way that would shock today – a different kind of poor – the real knot in the belly hunger type of poor. What they had – sometimes – what I had for a short time was work – not that it made us rich or anything, but it gave us routine – and a sense of belonging to something. But the work was so hard there was no time left for anything else. Sleep, work, eat. Sleep, work, eat. What kind of life is that?

I looked forward to not working at all – doing nothing – I looked forward to that until the day she died – my wife.

Everyone expects the man to die first – but cancer takes no notice of what people expect – it just does its work. Lots of people round here get cancer, it's in the water – the air – the mud. You've got no control over it. When I think back – I've not had control over anything. And that's a question in my head – what kind of men – are we if we have no control over anything that happens? Well, I just accept it now – I don't fight it anymore. I have no control – no power – that's it.

That's why I was lucky to find a new wife. I thought, 'she'd be good for us', a last throw of the dice.

I had good intentions – I am a good man. I don't mind saying it – whatever you might think – will think. I had good – intentions.

Grethel made an effort – tried to be nice – smiling – but not Hansel. I tell you straight I don't understand my son. I don't understand the world he lives in. He's either stuck in front of a computer – or out – with friends I never meet – and if I do I don't like the look of them because they look like him. Like shit. When I see him my blood boils – he's a loner – a misfit.

I still try sometimes – I say to him – I say –

Have a drink son – with your old man.

I don't want a drink – not with you.

He doesn't say that – out loud – it's just in his eyes – like a bloody troll he is – red eyes staring at me – as if I'm to blame. They say I'm fit for work now – but I'm not – I know I'm not. And if I went back to work – some crappy job – I'd get less than I do on benefits. I stay out of work for the good of the family.

Hansel?

HANSEL   What?

What are you doing – sneaking around like that?

HANSEL   I'm going out.

Out? There's no point in asking him – even when I'm sober. He likes his little secrets does Hansel. He's like a clam. Grethel isn't much better – though she's sweet enough – but I have to say the school is right – she's not normal – lives in another world. Grethel doesn't watch TV – she glares at it – and suddenly – just when I'm going out myself she says –

GRETHEL   Can I have a story?

A story? You've been watching stories all day long on TV. I'm going for a drink.

GRETHEL   Can I come with you?

Sure. Why not – you're my little girl aren't you.

HANSEL   You can't take her there.

That's right I say – very true – you stay here Grethel with your big brother – he'll look after you. He's got nothing else to do.

After that he just gives me one of those stares. Troll face. He thinks he's hard. Ha! I've seen his hands shake – he can't even lift a coke or a smoke without his hands shaking.

STEPMOTHER   It's time you left home.

Me?

STEPMOTHER   No not you – Hansel! A young man like that can't be hanging around the house all day. He's got to get out – get busy – move on.

GRETHEL   I don't want Hansel to go.

STEPMOTHER   And after that – it'll be your turn Grethel. Come sixteen you're out too. There's not enough money coming in for the four us – fact of life.

Grethel looks at me – but I can't say anything.

HANSEL   Fags and booze cost money.

STEPMOTHER   Did you hear that, husband? The sword of judgement – coming down on our skulls. Well – it's time you two got real – we're not here just to look after you – provide you with food and shelter – we've got our lives to live too. This house isn't yours you know.

GRETHEL   Yes it is.

STEPMOTHER   Oh? What have you paid for Grethel? Nothing. You cost money you do and lots of it. Look at him staring, husband – as if he'd like to chop us up into a thousand bits.

HANSEL   Maybe I will.

STEPMOTHER   What did you say?

HANSEL   You heard.

My wife stares at me as if I should shout something back – like, 'show us some respect you little good for nothing'. But what's the point?

I drink a lot that night and later my wife says to me –

STEPMOTHER   There must be more to life. I mean you see other people don't you – getting away – pulling away in big cars – dragging caravans – going on their travels – to hot sunny places. That's the life you promised me, husband – and I believed you – and what have I got – this – and it's those kids that hold us back – you know I'm right – a millstone around our necks they are – whatever you say.

But I don't say anything – too much bother –

STEPMOTHER   I'd do anything to get that life.

She says and looks at me –

STEPMOTHER   Anything.

4 STEPMOTHER

I had a little girl once –

I looked after her pretty well – but they still took her away – I had no say in the matter.

Well, after that I had other kids and they took them too.

But I didn't cry for them – not like I did the first one.

They said they were – in danger. Undernourished.

I thought life would get better with him –

Two of us against the world – and him with a good job – at the time – until he lost it drinking and driving – no really – driving along with a can of beer in his hand – using his knees to steer the car. He even offered the policeman a drink. Idiot.

And I believed all the things he said he was going to do for me.

Promised me the world – so I tried to be nice to the kids – though I never hit it off with Hansel.

I gave him things – like smokes and stuff but I think he just threw them away – or sold them.

That's more his style – he's scheming – you can see it in his eyes

He thinks he's above the rest of us – if only he could see himself – in his hood – Ha.

And as for Grethel – she's just plain weird –

I tell you I can't get through to her and actually – I don't really care.

They're not my fault are they? Not my kids.

I should have known – I did inside – that you can't replace 'mother'.

I can't stand that woman – I know she's dead – but I still can't stand her.

Husband keeps a dress of hers in the wardrobe – which is a bit weird I think – so I tried to throw it out – but he wouldn't let me and I tried more than once.

It was Hansel who caught me – stuffing it into a black bin liner in the kitchen.

And then Grethel and husband come in and they all just stare at me –

Like I was the devil.

Its funny then isn't it? Ironic – that's the word

That it falls to me to save this little lot – this wreckage

To whom I've got no connection at all – not really. But how?

We buy a lottery ticket every week don't we – and we watch others win and buy big houses and waste every penny – some of them do.

All they want is gold taps in the kitchen – things like that.

I'm not saying I wouldn't buy things – but I wouldn't waste it – the chance – to escape – somewhere warm.

The thing is – I'm not a cold climate person. The cold hangs round this city as if the sky were just a big damp kitchen cloth draped over everything. I blame the trees – they surround the place like they're laying us to siege.

I need to get out – not die here – in this place – with nothing.

When he lost his job – and started to drink – like he does now – I was going to leave – just walk out – but then I saw something on telly – and I had an idea. I told my cousin about it – I think he's a cousin and he laughed like a drain – but then he just said – Okay. Why not?

Hansel and Grethel don't know my cousin – no one does – that's the beauty of it.

PART THREE

Looking for Grethel

1 GRETHEL

The place where he kept me didn't frighten me – not at first – because he'd made it cosy

And he showed it to me – like on those TV programmes where someone is shown round a new house

This is the kitchen – which is well-appointed – 'appointed'.

This is the master bedroom and the en suite, 'en suite' it was like that.

In a way it was exciting because it was like being shown a secret place – a house beneath a house

And he showed me how you went through one room – into another one.

And from the outside you wouldn't know it was there at all.

The room was small and had a sink and a toilet in it – there were no windows

But I didn't say anything about that.

He wasn't nasty to me – and the first time he spoke to me I thought he had a nice voice

COUSIN – Hi Grethel – what are you doing out here – it's a bit late?

I'm looking for my brother

COUSIN – Oh Hansel. Would you like a sweet?

He offers me a sweet – it has purple wrapping. <u>I take one – two – three. He laughs.</u>

COUSIN – That's okay have as many as you want. Do you want me to take you home Grethel?

I want to find Hansel.

COUSIN – Can you keep a secret Grethel?

Yes.

COUSIN – I know where he is – Hansel is a friend of mine.

Where is he?

COUSIN – He's at my house

Why?

COUSIN – That's the secret part. Promise not to tell.

<u>I nod</u>

COUSIN   – Okay – he's got into some trouble – like he did before – with the police – so he can't come home for a little bit. Don't tell anyone will you?

No. How long will he be away?

COUSIN   – He doesn't know – that's why he sent me here – to find you. He wants to tell you that he's alright. He'll come home as soon as he can.

I want to see him

COUSIN   – That's not possible

I want to see him now.

COUSIN   – But it's late Grethel.

I don't care.

COUSIN   – You'd have to come to my house.

Where is your house?

COUSIN   – Not far – not by car. It's in the forest.

I want Hansel.

COUSIN   – Okay – then I'll take you – if it's what you really want. But first I should phone your mother to tell her.

She's not my mother.

COUSIN   – Your stepmother.

<u>He makes the call – but he turns away so I don't hear what he says.</u> Then he offers me his hand and I take it.

I don't know how long the drive is. There's a blanket on the back seat and he says I can lie down and have a sleep and that's what I do. When I wake up I'm already inside his house. He must have carried me in the blanket.

Where are we?

COUSIN   – At my place.

Where's Hansel?

COUSIN – I don't know – he must have gone out. You can wait in here. Oh – do you have a mobile?

Yes

COUSIN – Can I borrow it – I'm out of credit?

I left it at home.

COUSIN – Oh.

Then he brings me some more sweets and we watch telly together. I keep asking about Hansel and after a while he seems to get annoyed and goes out. He locks the door behind him. I watched the telly and there's a film on with bad people doing bad things to each other and I shut my eyes. I start to cry then cos I know that I'd been tricked – and I cry and cry.

2 HANSEL

Stepmother says –

STEPMOTHER Don't call Grethel's friends till the morning. Some people have to work you know –

So I wait till eight but they haven't seen her. Dad comes in – looks like a ghost. She glares at him and I can see something in her eyes – but I can't tell what it is.

FATHER I feel – awful – bloody awful. What?

Grethel's missing.

FATHER What?

STEPMOTHER He said Grethel hasn't come home.

Her phone rings – she answers it. We wait.

Who was it?

STEPMOTHER A call centre – India –somewhere.

FATHER Where is she?

STEPMOTHER We don't know.

I'll call the police.

STEPMOTHER No I'll call the police.

I watch her dial – and she takes a deep breath – and her voice changes.

STEPMOTHER It's my little girl – my stepdaughter – she's not come home – and I'm terribly worried.

I know something isn't right but there's no time because then it starts first the police – Where were you last night? Out – alone. Where? Looking for Grethel. Within hours people we barely know are sending messages of sympathy. When I go outside – someone takes a photo of me – doesn't even ask. Word has got round – a missing child. By the evening it's on the local TV and there's our house – with the smashed front window and the scrubby garden the local cats use as a toilet. The next morning it's on national TV – Next thing local people get together and search the area – Stepmother smiles a lot – thanks them – looks as if she might cry. She appears on telly –

STEPMOTHER I just want you to know Grethel – if you can hear me – that I really miss you and if you've run away – are hiding somewhere – with someone – it's alright don't be frightened – you've done nothing wrong – just come home – please come home.

Father speaks too – he reads out his piece and won't look at the camera –

FATHER   If anyone has seen, or knows where my daughter is – I urge them to come forward – take pity on her and on us. Come forward please.

The papers say stepmother is emotional, and that father is cold and distant.

The police come back to the house –

Where did you look Hansel? When you were looking for Grethel – what did you see?

I stare at them.

What did you see? Nothing.

I run to the mine – climb the ladder – nothing? Sit on the ledge. Stare at the city – NOTHING? But I did see something – I saw Grethel taken by a shadow – at a distance of a thousand yards? But what good is that? And what if news got out that I had seen someone take her – then that someone might – do something he never planned to do – just to cover his tracks. And he might do that anyway – cos isn't that what happens – when little girls go missing? No. NO! I have to have time to find her – me – no one else. I have to work it out because I know something isn't right – not with stepmother and more terrifying – not with father. Think – think.

I climb back down and stand where Grethel had stood – reaching out her hand – for what?

I shine a light from my phone on to the ground and I see a sweet wrapper – purple – and a few yards away <u>another sweet wrapper</u> – Did she drop them? Is that what I saw, Grethel tempted away by a man with sweets? Grethel wouldn't do that. I've told her so many times. Did she know this person?

I walk – toward the road – through the playground – past the crocodile. I reach the road – it's dimly lit – there's only one place to park. I walk to it – look down. There in the gutter is another sweet – this time it's not opened. Grethel has left me a clue – a trail – but if she went in a car – then it was no good – no good.

3 GRETHEL

He says a week has passed – but I can't tell. I cried a lot at first and screamed. He said

COUSIN You sound like a cat

And slapped my face.

COUSIN There's no point in screaming – because we're deep in the woods. No one can hear.

Every day he brings me sweets, nothing else – and I feel ill all the time. He thinks this is funny – I ask for other food – but he doesn't seem to understand. He says

COUSIN   Kids live on sweets don't they?

I watch telly all day long, not news – just cartoons. After seven days my little head begins to spin 'like a top'. I don't understand that 'like a top' but I've heard the words. Every day he gets a bit more angry and leaves me alone for hours and hours. I know something bad has happened because Hansel hasn't come. I sit on the bed and dream a lot. I dream that this isn't happening to me – not to me – it's happening to someone else who looks like me. I imagine this person so fiercely that after a while I begin to see her sitting on the end of the bed. When I wave she waves back. I stick out my tongue and she sticks out her tongue and that makes me smile – but she doesn't smile – which is strange. I talk to her for a long time and she listens very carefully and I tell her not to worry – Hansel will come and save her. He is the only one in the world who will come. At first the little girl who looks like me vanished sometimes – but every day she becomes a little bit more real – although she's not real – I know that – she's not made out of skin and bone like me. I have stopped crying so much because now she does all the crying and I sit on the end of the bed and watch her – and yesterday she was sick on all those sweets. Poor little girl.

4 HANSEL

Dad is staring at the TV.

I look at him and he glances away. He's been drinking. I say –

Have they found her?

FATHER   No – they think she's dead.

He smiles.

What's funny about that?

FATHER   Nothing Hansel – don't fret. She's not dead.

How do you know?

STEPMOTHER   He means – he just knows – feels it – cos he's her father.

I stare at her.

STEPMOTHER   If they find her – you'll be the first to know Hansel. Here –

Then she gives me some money.

What's that for?

STEPMOTHER   Being a good boy.

Where'd you get it?

STEPMOTHER   A gift. You don't look a gift horse in the mouth – do you Hansel?

I go upstairs and watch TV. I watch programmes I never knew existed. Programmes where people in suits just sit and talk – and now they're talking about us – and they go on and on.

5 STEPMOTHER

To be honest – it's nice to have some attention – I mean – what's wrong with that? It's why people go on Big Brother isn't it – it's not just to do with the money – it's to be seen – My God – it's to be known – proof that you even bloody exist.

They've been out collecting money in tins – and they bring it round to the house and give it me – and then there's the post. Cash, just coming through the door. It's amazing how generous people have been – stupid I say. I wouldn't send my hard-earned money to strangers. It keeps flooding in though – just like I said it would and lo and behold 'Husband' is happier than I've seen him for a long time. I swear he doesn't miss Grethel – not that he's heartless – it's just – she was kind of absent anyway. It's odd though how a little money can lift the spirits – a strange kind of magic – that's worked on him.

6 HANSEL

They say things like – we're the new poor –

Downstairs they're laughing.

That we're useless.

Downstairs they're laughing.

Hopeless. I am not useless – I am not hopeless. I will find Grethel and prove you wrong.

I kick the TV and it goes off.

FATHER   Alright son?

No – I'm not alright – are you alright?

FATHER   Keep your hair on. I was just asking. Here – here's a little cash. Go on take it – buy yourself something – anything.

STEPMOTHER   Like a haircut.

She says. They laugh then.

STEPMOTHER   Or a sense of humour.

FATHER   No really son – take it – take it. On the house.

I take it – stare at it.

Thanks.

STEPMOTHER   There's something you ought to know Hansel.

What?

STEPMOTHER   You tell him – you're his father.

FATHER   We had a phone call from the police about Grethel – didn't we love.

STEPMOTHER   We did.

FATHER   But It's nothing – you're not to be worried.

What do you mean?

FATHER   They've stopped searching – two weeks now – so they called it off – phoned to tell us. But it doesn't mean – does it love – it doesn't mean – anything. You're not to worry son.

Not to worry?

She cuffs him round the head – like he was a kid – and they laugh suddenly. She sees me watching and says.

STEPMOTHER   Things will work out Hansel – here have a sweet.

She holds out her hand – and there it is – a sweet – with a purple wrapping

What are you staring at? Why's he always staring?

FATHER   Hansel? Hansel?

Running now – running.

7 HANSEL

Back across the empty field – through the place she'd stood, reaching out her hand.

Climbing – through the iron hoops and sit knees to chin, face in hands, hands in fists.

Uncurl and hold the purple sweet.

Eyes blind, head blank, so full of noise I hardly hear the thought that somewhere there's a secret –

Somewhere there's a clue that leads to Grethel.

Running – Running back across the empty field – through the place she'd stood reaching out her hand –

Then I see Father, coming down the side of the park and throw myself to the ground. When I stand I watch the back of his head moving away – he's talking to himself, muttering like something has slipped in his brain – a cog undone. He staggers slightly – stumbling forward – gone.

Up again – I run, and when I reach the door my hands are shaking. In the kitchen I push sugar into my mouth. One spoon, three, four, just to stop the shaking.

Breathe now as deeply as I can, stifle a cough because I see smoke rising through the glass of the back door. She's sitting behind it, on the back step surrounded by fag ends – and she's so deep in them she doesn't know I'm there.

Slip off trainers and creep up stairs – cat up no good – notice for the first time how shabby the stairs are – carpet threadbare, dangerous.

Outside their room – stop – never been in their room – never wanted to be in their room

I push against the door and step in. It's odd, nothing much has changed – it looks the same. Then I see someone else and draw breath – but it's only me in the mirror, the boy in the hood, looking for Grethel.

I slide the wardrobe door open and step back unnerved. A red dress is floating there, silent – alone – A dress mother wore on special nights. I breathe in and catch her scent and before I know what I'm doing I have my face in the dress and it does – it really smells of her.

STEPMOTHER   Hansel?

Freeze

STEPMOTHER   Hansel are you there?

I step inside the wardrobe, next to the dress.

STEPMOTHER   Is anyone there? Hansel?

Through a crack in the door I can see her, sitting on the bed – thinking. After a time she reaches beneath the bed and pulls something out.

A suitcase. Blue.

She stands in front of it – opens it – and I can see her staring down into it, almost expressionless, then she puts her hand into it and picks up a pile of bank notes – picks them up like they were flowers – and smells them, suddenly pressing them against her face, rubbing the money into her skin. Then she – nods to herself – as if she's made a decision.

8 GRETHEL

When I wave she waves back. I stick out my tongue and she sticks out her tongue and that makes me smile – but she doesn't smile – which is strange. She says –

Where is he?

Who?

The man.

I don't know.

He hasn't been to see us for so long.

How long?

Do you think he'll ever come back?

I don't know

I don't think he will.

I poke out my tongue. She pokes out hers – then says –

Everything will be alright, won't it?

Yes.

Liar.

Yes.

LIAR. I feel sick.

I'm sorry.

It's not your fault – it's Hansel's.

Don't you talk about Hansel.

Where is he then?

He's busy – he has to go to college.

Liar.

He has to – every day.

Liar.

Stop it!

HANSEL!

He can't hear you – no one can hear you.

I know that.

Then there's no point in shouting is there! Shh – he's coming.

Hansel?

No – the man.

COUSIN   – What are you shouting for? I told you not to shout.

I wasn't – it was her.

COUSIN   – Who ?

Her – at the end of the bed.

COUSIN   – Who's at the end of the bed?

My friend – the one who shouts and is sick.

COUSIN   – There's no one there – I told you that before too.

You can't see her – you can't see her – you can't see her.

COUSIN   – Shut up! Shut up! –

He's about to hit the poor little girl at the end of the bed <u>when the phone rings –</u>

9 HANSEL

<u>She waits – patient – calm – for the phone to be answered.</u>

STEPMOTHER   It's me.

COUSIN   – Six o'clock, you told me six o'clock. Where the hell have you been?

STEPMOTHER   I have to wait till the house is empty.

COUSIN   – Six o'clock – that's what you said. If there's someone in the house then go out of the house – but phone me at six – at six.

STEPMOTHER   I can't just go out – not anymore.

COUSIN   – You don't know what it's like here

STEPMOTHER   There are people everywhere, with cameras.

COUSIN   – Waiting for the phone to ring.

STEPMOTHER   They'll want to know who I'm phoning – what I'm saying. You don't want them to know that do you?

COUSIN   – So?

STEPMOTHER   So?

COUSIN   So how much longer?

STEPMOTHER   How is she?

COUSIN   – Sick.

STEPMOTHER   Sick?

COUSIN   – That's what I said – sick.

STEPMOTHER   Are you feeding her?

COUSIN   – 'Course I'm feeding her.

10 GRETHEL

He throws some sweets hard at the other little girl at the end of the bed.

STEPMOTHER   What kind of sick?

COUSIN   – Physically – it stinks in here – and she's gone all strange – talking to herself –

STEPMOTHER   She always does that – it's normal.

COUSIN　　　　– Normal? – She gives me the spooks. I can't take much more of her – and her invisible friend – I'm not used to children am I.

STEPMOTHER　Just stay calm – it'll be worth it.

COUSIN　　　　– Two weeks you said – at the most.

STEPMOTHER　I know what I said – I said we had to be flexible – we had to wait and see – and the longer we wait the more money comes in – alright. Alright?

COUSIN　　　　– Alright – but how much longer?

STEPMOTHER　I don't know – this whole thing is different – different to what I thought – it's – bigger.

COUSIN　　　　– What do you mean – bigger?

STEPMOTHER　If Grethel comes back she'll get a lot of attention. They told me they'd take her to a special unit – for screening – that's the word they used – screening – they'll take her and ask her questions about what's happened.

COUSIN　　　　– So?

STEPMOTHER　So that changes everything – doesn't it – unless you want to go back to prison?

COUSIN　　　　– Why should I go back to prison? No one knows me – no one knows I'm involved.

STEPMOTHER　She does.

He smiles at the other girl. He's been eating something yellow and has bits of food in his teeth.

COUSIN　　　　– What are you talking about?

STEPMOTHER　Just listen.

COUSIN　　　　– I'm listening – I just don't get what you're saying.

STEPMOTHER　They'll be all over us – like flies on shit – that's what I'm saying – so I'm just thinking – thinking it through – slowly – calmly for my sake – for yours.

COUSIN   – For Christ's sake I can't keep her here for ever can I? – Hello?

STEPMOTHER   No – so we have to think it through – again.

COUSIN   – Stop crying. Stop crying.

STEPMOTHER   You're in there with her?

COUSIN   – Yes.

STEPMOTHER   I told you not to do that. I told you.

COUSIN   – It's not my fault – it's yours – for not calling me at six. Stop crying. I can't – I won't – I mean I can't go back to prison.

STEPMOTHER   I know.

COUSIN   – No you don't know.

STEPMOTHER   But I do know this – if she comes back – that's where we both end up – you understand what I'm saying now?

COUSIN   This was never what we talked about. Never. I can't – I just – can't –

STEPMOTHER   Can't what? It's not like you have to do anything.

COUSIN   – What do you mean?

STEPMOTHER   You built the room – it's what you're good at isn't it. That's what you told me.

COUSIN   – So?

STEPMOTHER   So you built it – and no one even knows you built it. No one knows it's there. And that's why no one's found her even though they've been searching – thousands of people searching and not finding because no one knows that room is there – do they?

COUSIN   – No.

STEPMOTHER   So you don't have to do anything – except close the door. Just close the door.

COUSIN   – Just close the door?

STEPMOTHER   You can close a door can't you?

11 HANSEL

She puts the phone down cool as you like – <u>closes the suitcase and puts it back under the bed – puts the phone in the drawer beside the bed and goes downstairs.</u>

Running now, in my hand – I've got the phone. The phone which has only called one number –

Across the empty field right through the place Grethel had stood reaching out to take his hand – the hand of the man at the end of the phone. Across and to my right, by the kebab shop there's a police car, its blue light spinning in the night. Two officers by the shop entrance talking to some boys. I'll go right up and give them the phone, they'll know what to do, how to trace the call, and by daybreak Grethel will be found – alive.

Officer!

One of the officers – a woman – turns and sees me coming out of the shadows, hood down, moving with purpose toward them – holding something out in front – a shout

Stay there!

Drop it. Drop it!

But I can't drop the phone – I can't. It's the clue – It's – now her hand is reaching to her gun, and the other kids are shouting –

And suddenly the officers are kicked and punched and I'm standing there in the dark with my hood down, hand out and the boys are running past me –

Run. Run.

Pulling my sleeve and yelling with glee.

Run. Run.

And the officer is coming towards me and I turn and run – run.

12 HANSEL

The papers say I look like something the devil cooked up for dinner

Don't like the way I hide my face with a hood

Don't like the way I cling to the shadows

To the side of the street – like a cat – up to no good.

I sit on the ledge, looking down at the field – the phone in my hand.

I put the phone to my ear – breathe deeply – try to slow my heart. The phone rings, once, twice, three times – he's not expecting a call.

COUSIN   – What is it? – Hello? – Who's there?

I have something for you.

COUSIN   – Who's this?

And you have something for me – a girl.

The phone slams down and in my head I can see him, pacing the floor, panicking. I count to ten and call again. He answers – listens. I can hear his breath. I say

A girl called Grethel.

COUSIN   – I don't know what you're talking about.

She's sick.

COUSIN   – How do you know she's been sick? Who is this?

I know everything, that's why it's important you listen. Are you listening?

COUSIN   – Hansel? It's you, isn't it? Well – Hansel, you don't know what you're doing, what you're dealing with. You have no idea.

The money will be in a suitcase.

COUSIN   – What money?

Your money. In a suitcase and if you don't do exactly what I say –
you won't get it, ever.

COUSIN   – Go on.

If you want your money bring Grethel back to the same place you
found her. The exact place.

COUSIN   – You saw?

At the same time – 11.30 – tonight.

COUSIN   – Wait, wait, the exact place?

Bring a torch, you'll see the suitcase – it's blue.

I put the phone down, and bend over – feel like retching, but I'm
still thinking and he's thinking too. He's thinking about how I
got the number – he's not thinking that I've got the phone – so
I'm thinking he'll call back thinking that she will answer. <u>The
phone rings.</u>

Hello?

You don't want to go to prison do you?

This time the phone goes dead – quietly. Now I can feel him,
stamping the floor, hitting the wall. Perhaps Grethel can hear
him. I don't run now – I creep, crawl, a shadow on the wall of the
house. Try not to shake as I open the door. Take off my trainers
like before. Move towards the stairs.

STEPMOTHER   Where's the phone?

<u>I turn slowly. She's standing there, fag in one hand a big kitchen
knife in the other. I say –</u>

What phone?

STEPMOTHER   My phone – the one you took from the bedroom.

I haven't got your phone. Why should I have your phone?

STEPMOTHER   Same reason you're sneaking up the stairs in your
dirty socks – Like you did before – leaving your dirty trainers –
just there.

<u>We stare at each other.</u>

STEPMOTHER   Always sneaking around, pretending to be stupid, but you're not stupid are you Hansel.

She puts one foot on the stairs. I take one back.

STEPMOTHER   You're clever – and you're angry. I know you are, and I feel the same – exactly the same. Course I do. We've been held down – you and me Hansel, by people who are no better than us but who just happen to be born into some good luck, money – opportunities – chances – and they go to a good school don't they – and get a good job – and they make more money – and then they pass it on to their kids and on it goes, round and round but it never – ever – trickles down. Don't you believe it will – cos it won't, it's a lie. So you and me – we have to make our own way as best we can – we have to work our own chances – and here's the thing Hansel – I'm going to give you a chance, on a plate. And you be clever now – cos in this world it's the only one you're going to get.

I don't know what you're talking about.

STEPMOTHER   Yes you do. You've been watching, listening, staring – taking it all in.

She takes another step. I take one back.

STEPMOTHER   And now you've got some sort of plan and I'm here to save you from it. Do what I say and I'll save us all.

Where's Grethel?

STEPMOTHER   Grethel? She's safe – in a safe place and she's our ticket Hansel – our chance. Unless you want to be poor for the rest of your life that is – unless you want to put your own father behind bars for the rest of his. You don't want that – do you – Hansel?

No.

STEPMOTHER   Then give me the phone – and I'll give you a fair share of what we've made – as a family. Give it me – now.

She doesn't see him. She doesn't even feel his presence. Because she's locked on me, like a missile and Dad's behind her with a great lump of wood and for a drunk he's surprisingly quiet – so she never senses it coming down. It hits her with a horrible thud that would have made me sick at any other time. She falls – and Dad drops the timber – and on his knees he's whimpering –

FATHER   I'm sorry. I'm sorry.

Sorry?

FATHER   Tell Grethel – I'm sorry. I'm sorry.

He breaks down.

Phone the police Dad – they'll listen to you. Phone the police – can you do that?

FATHER   She was going to kill her. She was going to kill my little girl. I never meant, I never thought – I never –

Just phone the police.

Running. Climbing.

11.35. Sitting on the ledge. He's not here – he's not coming. I've failed. I'm stupid and useless and – and then I see a shape moving slowly through the kid's play area. It waits for a moment – holding something in its arms. It's him – it must be him. He stops – looks around just like before. Then he puts down the bundle. Grethel? A torch comes on and the beam searches – falling on the blue suitcase. The torch swings round again, and then rests – he kneels by the suitcase – is about to open it when his phone rings. I say –

You haven't got time.

He looks up and sees blue lights flashing and hears sirens getting louder – and he's off and running towards the trees – and I'm running too towards the dark shape on the floor. Stay calm, stay calm. All I can see is a blanket. I pull it up. Grethel? Nothing. He's tricked me and I scream –

GRETHEL! GRETHEL!

GRETHEL   Hansel?

Her voice is so small it makes me shudder. I turn and there she is, standing – white as a ghost and falling, falling but I catch her and hold her and tears come out of me from a place I didn't know existed and I'm no longer – poor.

PART FOUR

Aftermath – Four Points of View

1 FATHER

At first I was in agony. You can get most things in here, but you can't get a drink. I'm sober now, of course – dead sober. There's a telly in here. They had Hansel, my Hansel on the telly – on the main news staring out – like he always does – and I looked at him a long time – and I thought – I thought he looked like his mother – that's what I thought – he has her face – her features. You know what they said about my son? Said he was a hero, who had overcome his terrible upbringing – that's right – his terrible upbringing.

They come and look at me once every hour to see I haven't killed myself. Sometimes I think I might.

Had time to think. Loads of it – so I go over and over the same ground – and I still don't know – I really don't know how I ever did what I did. I'm not like these other criminals in here – who set out to hurt people. I set out to – to work – bring up a family – but that's what happens, you slide, you slip, you fall and suddenly you don't know, who you are, what you're doing. Not till it's too late.

One day they sent Grethel. They said she wanted to see me. And when she saw me she smiled, and I hung my head. I hung my head.

2 STEPMOTHER

I don't care what you think.

I don't care what you think!

That's what I scream from behind the bars, so it echoes down the corridor.

I don't care.

They've put me in solitary because some of the other lags have put a price on my head, ten cigarettes, for the one who gets me. Ten ciggies, in here that makes you rich – and they shout out

I'm going to get you.

One day –

When you're not looking.

Monster.

That's what they think I am. First day inside this girl says to me – how could you do it – a little girl – you're a monster. That's right I said and don't you forget it and I held her look. I held it till she had to look away. So I'm in solitary. They sent a woman to talk to me once a week to check the state of my mental health. She says to me, tell me about your childhood. Why I says? But after three weeks I got fed up of not saying anything so just to fill the space I told her – I can't remember anything – but then it came to me – a memory – and I told her. I remember waking up – there was no one in the house. I had brothers – half brothers and sisters but god knows where they all were. Must have gone out – and someone had taped the windows over so it was always dark and the front door was locked. I went into each room to see if anyone was there – but there wasn't. Eventually I got hungry so I climbed up on a chair to look in the cupboard but there was nothing in it – no plates – nothing. But then I found an old packet of cornflakes – in one of the bedrooms – I think it was cornflakes and I ate that. I couldn't understand why no one came home – I wasn't going to cry though cos no one likes that. I was there for a week I suppose – it's hard to tell – in the end I finished the corn flakes and then I ate the box – which is funny really cos there's not much difference – taste wise.

The woman just stared at me and then she asked me what it felt like – being taken into care – and she was writing down what I was saying in a note book in front of her. But I was tired of talking by that time – tired of her face, all made up and pretty. It made me want to smash it – which I tried to do so she never came back again.

I watch TV fifteen hours a day and afterwards I can't remember any of it – and when I'm not watching TV I talk to myself – think about what I'm going to do when I get out of prison.

Everything will be alright – won't it?

Yes.

Tell me everything will be alright.

It will be I promise.

How do you know?

Because my money will be waiting for me won't it – in a blue suitcase

Waiting for you?

Yeah – because they never caught him did they. Never knew who he was.

He'll have spent it –

No he won't because he's scared of me, and he should be too – very scared. He knows that money is mine – it's my ticket, my chance, my future. I deserve a future – same as anyone. Same as you.

3 HANSEL

They let me see Grethel every couple of weeks. She's been taken in by a nice family – that's what they said – she'll be with a nice family. It'll be good for her. She said –

GRETHEL   I don't want to go.

But she didn't have much choice –

GRETHEL   Hansel?

I'll come and see you.

GRETHEL   Promise?

Of course –

So I went to see her and the nice family and we all sat down together to eat round a big table. Grethel was getting used to it by then, sitting down for dinner – talking. They talked so much it did my head in. I had to pull my hood right up over my head so they wouldn't talk to me. Then Grethel threw a piece of potato at me and it fell on the carpet – and they all stopped talking then – and me and Grethel looked at them and we laughed. We really laughed like we hadn't laughed in years.

4 HANSEL AND GRETHEL

GRETHEL   Hansel comes to see me sometimes. I'm not sure how often because I have trouble with time. I wish Hansel was always here. I ask him to stay but he says –

HANSEL   I have to go to college.

GRETHEL   So I sit in my room – it's a nice room with a window and sometimes – the other girl who looks just like me – and cries a lot and is always unhappy – sometimes she comes and sits on the end of the bed like she did in that place. But these days she doesn't come as often – so I have more time just to sit and stare out of the window and dream and dream and dream –

HANSEL   Do you want to go for a walk?

GRETHEL   Where?

HANSEL   In the woods

GRETHEL   I don't like woods – they're scary.

HANSEL   Even if I'm there?

GRETHEL   No – not if you're there.

HANSEL   Come on then –but put a coat on – it's getting cold.

GRETHEL   What about the nice family?

HANSEL   We'll be back by morning.

GRETHEL   Now we are in the woods and there's frost on the ground and I like the sound it makes when you walk on it. As we go further there are more and more trees – I don't want to go any further.

HANSEL   You don't have to – we're here.

GRETHEL   Where?

HANSEL   Special place.

GRETHEL   Now Hansel's got a spade. Where he got it from I don't know but he's digging with it and out of the ground comes a big black bin liner which he empties onto the forest floor. What is it?

HANSEL   It's money Grethel – your money – lots of it.

GRETHEL   My money?

HANSEL   The money everyone gave to help find you. So I reckon it's yours. If I leave it here in the ground it'll rot.

GRETHEL   What shall we do with it?

HANSEL   I don't know – what do you want to do?

GRETHEL   I don't know – what do you want to do?

HANSEL   You could buy lots of things.

GRETHEL   You could buy lots of things.

HANSEL   Like what?

GRETHEL   Clothes and things – I don't know. All the things people buy when they have money. <u>Hansel sits by the money and stares at it. After a time he reaches into his college bag.</u> What's this?

HANSEL   A sandwich – made it for you.

GRETHEL   A picnic?

HANSEL   Yeah – a picnic in the woods.

GRETHEL   It's too cold for a picnic.

HANSEL   Yeah – I suppose it is really. I just thought – you might be hungry.

GRETHEL   I'm eating the sandwich which Hansel has made for me and suddenly there's a nice big fire to keep us warm – and the pretty flames – light up our faces and the trees too so they don't look scary anymore, and we kneel by the fire in the forest and have our picnic. Hansel –

HANSEL   And Grethel.

The end.

Production Images

Theatr Iolo production of *Missing*.

Lucy Rivers as Grethel and John North as the Cousin.

Caroline Bunce as the Stepmother.

Consol theatre production of *Looking for Grethel.*

Standing – Tobias Novo as Hansel.

Eva Hortsman as the Stepmother and
Markus Kirschbaum as the Father.

Hanna Charlotte Kruger as Grethel.

PIRATES!

This play was a joint commission by the Polka Theatre London and Imagination Stage Washington USA. The Polka production opened at the Polka Theatre, Wimbledon, on June 19th, 2010, and the Imagination Stage production, 'Pirates – a Boy at Sea' opened at Imagination Stage, Bethesda, Washington USA on June 23rd, 2010.

Suitable for everyone aged 6 and above.

Pirates! won a 'Distinguished play award' in 2012 from the American Alliance for Theatre and Education.

UK Director Jonathan Lloyd, Designer Liz Cooke, Music/Sound James Grant.

US Director Janet Stanford, Designer Tom Donahue, Costume Designer Brandon R. McWilliams.

Characters	**UK**	**US**
Jim	Edward Dede	Josh Sticklin
Captain Freely/Mum	Rachel Nott	Colleen Delany
Captain McGovern/Dad	Tunde Makinde	Tim Getman
Sneep	Ben Sewell	Michael John Casey
Harry	Michael Sewell	Phillip Reid

Two sharks *(played by Captains Freely and McGovern)*

Cast size

Five.

Notes

Sneep and Harry can either be played by two men, two women, or one of each.

This text of Pirates! is as produced by the Polka theatre company, London. There were slight dialogue variations in the American production: 'Mum' became 'Mom' and 'Jim Jams' became 'PJ's'. For the sharks, 'new Volks – wagen – camp – er – van' became 'rec – re – ational – vehicle' and 'mucking about' became 'fooling around'. Verse two of the 'Searching endlessly' song was also adjusted:

And we'll down our grog and spend our tin
And freely go on a freshening wind
Searching endlessly
And we'll wake all night and sleep all day
There ain't no rules that we obey
Searching endlessly.

Act 1

Scene 1: Treasure Lost

Scene 2: Kidnapped

Scene 3: On the *Horizon*

Scene 4: The Captain's Cabin

Scene 5: Battle Stations

Act 2

Scene 1: A Sea Battle

Scene 2: Boy Overboard

Scene 3: An English Man-o'-War

Scene 4: Storm at Sea

Scene 5: Treasure Found

ACT ONE, SCENE ONE

Treasure Lost

Enter Sneep wearing an eye patch and carrying a spade.

SNEEP   Harry? Harry? Harry!

Enter Harry.

HARRY   Yes Sneep.

SNEEP   Don't do that – sneaking up – like – like some kind of thief. Found anything?

HARRY   Rock and sand. Sand and rock.

SNEEP   You'd best tell the Captain.

HARRY   She won't be happy.

SNEEP   What are we to do? We've dug up every inch of this rotten little sandbank, and it's not here.

HARRY   Perhaps – you'd best tell the captain then.

SNEEP   I will too – cos I'm not scared of her. An' at times like this I think I'd make a better Captain than her. What say you to that?

HARRY   I say – I'll dig till sundown.

SNEEP   That's your trouble Harry – too loyal for your own good.

HARRY   And you – too cunning for yours! *(He digs furiously – and Sneep grabs the spade from him but he continues with his bare hands.)*

SNEEP   Give it up Harry. It's a waste of honest sweat. This treasure don't even exist, 'cept in wild tales and even wilder dreams. We've dug up an 'undred islands just like this one and be no richer for it. I'm a pirate Harry and I need to match the seeking with the finding. And I don't like digging, neither – *(As he speaks* *a treasure chest large enough to hold two people magically appears behind them)* – dig, dig, digging all day long – like we was moles underground. I like to be at sea Harry; the wind in me hair, salt on me tongue, sailing the big blue, a cutlass between me teeth and a pirate yell in me throat. And most of all I like capturing other people's ships, taking things that don't belong to me – like – like –

HARRY   Some kind of thief.

SNEEP   Exactly – stealing an' robbing an' nicking – cos I'm a pirate, a dyed in the wool, scarf round me head, patch on me eye – PIRATE!

HARRY   Sneep.

SNEEP   Which is nothing like a mole.

HARRY   Sneep.

SNEEP   In a hole

HARRY   SNEEP!

SNEEP   WHAT?

HARRY   It's there – the treasure chest – it's there.

Sneep looks slowly around, sees the chest and then looks slowly back to Harry.

SNEEP   Still there?

HARRY   Aye – out of nowhere.

Sneep looks back quickly.

SNEEP   I don't like this, not one bit of it.

HARRY   But we found the chest.

SNEEP   No Harry – it found us, and that's too odd for my liking. Don't touch it!

HARRY   Why not? We'll be rich – rich.

SNEEP   Or dead – dead. That chest is no common thing. It's cursed. See the words there.

HARRY What kind o' curse?

SNEEP How would I know? I can't read any more than you can think. Go find the Captain.

HARRY I'm right glad I've got you to look after me Sneep.

SNEEP That's fine Harry –

HARRY No I mean it – where would this dull Harry be without his clever Sneep – dead I say – dead.

SNEEP Don't get sentimental on me Harry – just go – go. *(Exit Harry. Sneep watches him leave and then utters a dark greedy sound. He hugs the chest. Music. He opens it and it is full of gold.)* Ha, ha, ha, ha, ha, aaaaah. *(Sneep writhes in ecstasy then starts to shove gold coins into his pockets. He hears Harry and Captain Freely approaching and closes the lid.)* Captain, Captain this way. *(Enter Captain Freely. She is a dashing pirate, very clearly a woman, but dressed as a man.)* See what I have found you. Ha!

FREELY Ha! Ha!

SNEEP Ha! Ha! Ha!

HARRY Ha! Ha! Ha! OH?

The Captain has a sword at Sneep's throat.

FREELY Did you open it?

SNEEP Me? On my life I never did.

HARRY Be careful Captain. Sneep says the chest is cursed – cursed.

FREELY Yes, and here are the words of it.
 'If you be a liar and have opened this lid
 You will perish here, for what – you – did.
 Empty your pockets on the count of three,
 Or die without hope – um – most painfully.'
 One, two –

Sneep empties his pockets rapidly.

HARRY   Sneep!

SNEEP   I didn't mean nothing by it – It was the gold, Captain – the gold made me do it – and I was powerless to resist.

FREELY   I know Sneep, I know, and that's because you are a proper, dyed in the wool –

SNEEP   Scarf round me head –

FREELY   Patch on yer eye –

SNEEP   Pirate.

FREELY (*grabs Sneep*) But steal from me again and I shall pluck out yer other eye and pickle it!

HARRY   Pickle his eye?

FREELY   IN VINEGAR! I will not be stolen from – you understand, the both of ya?

HARRY/SNEEP   Aye, Aye Cap'n.

FREELY   Now then, I wonder – who is Jim?

HARRY/SNEEP   Jim?

FREELY   That's what it says right here. (*Reads*) 'This chest belongs to Jim Watts.'

HARRY   Never heard of no Jim Watts.

SNEEP   You mean, that's what it says – in addition to – dying most painfully on the count of three?

FREELY   Of course Sneep, though oddly – those particular words seem to be vanishing before my very eyes, though there is another rhyme. (*She reads to herself.*) Of sorts.

HARRY   Vanishing words? 'Tis true then – the chest is cursed – CURSED!

FREELY   Don't overdo the cursing Harry. Well – Jim Watts – whoever you be – prepare to be robbed by PIRATES.

HARRY/SNEEP   Ha, ha!

HARRY   We can open it then?

FREELY   Yes Harry.

HARRY   You do it Sneep.

FREELY   Allow me.

Music. Captain Freely opens the lid. Music stops. The gold has vanished.

FREELY   Sneep?

SNEEP   On my life –

HARRY   Don't pickle his eye captain – I beg you.

FREELY   What have you done with my TREASURE?

SNEEP   Nothing – I just – had a peek – it was there and now – now – it's – it's – Look Captain – Look.

FREELY   Think I'll fall for that old trick do ya Sneep?

SNEEP   There's a ship – out to sea.

FREELY   Fetch the vinegar Harry.

SNEEP   But Captain – *(A boom of a cannon shot makes them duck.)* Told you.

HARRY   There Cap'n – an English man-o'-war.

FREELY   HMS *Vengeance*.

HARRY   They've sent out a landing craft.

SNEEP   And Captain McGovern is in it.

HARRY   He'll hang us all for sure.

SNEEP   We should run then – RUN! Cap'n?

FREELY   Aye Sneep – you run – run back to the ship, set sail and save it from the English navy.

SNEEP   What about you and Harry?

FREELY   We'll hold them back as long as we can, so that you can escape with your life and save the ship. We'll join you – on the *Horizon* – when we can.

SNEEP   Harry?

HARRY   Don't get sentimental on me – Sneep – not now.

FREELY   Go, go, go!

Exit Sneep.

HARRY   They're running up the beach captain.

FREELY   How many?

HARRY   About ten – or thirty – and they're waving their weapons and yelling something terrible. *(He turns to see Captain Freely getting into the chest.)* Captain?

FREELY   Fight 'em off Harry – as long as you can. That's my boy.

HARRY   Aye, Aye – Captain – long as I can.

She closes the lid and Sneep enters, not Sneep the pirate but Sneep the English sailor wearing a short blue regulation jacket. He attacks Harry and they fight. Sneep the English sailor gets wounded in the eye and yells out in agony – Harry is about to run him through when Captain McGovern enters and puts a sword to his chest. Captain McGovern wears a 'long tailed blue' – a coat denoting his rank.

MCGOVERN   Drop your cutlass – drop it!

Harry drops his cutlass.

MCGOVERN   Are you injured sailor?

SNEEP   Got me in the eye Cap'n – but I'll survive.

MCGOVERN *(to Harry)* Where is Captain Freely? Where is she?

HARRY   I will never betray my Captain – never – never – never.

MCGOVERN   Kill him.

HARRY   She's in the box!

MCGOVERN   Take him back to the ship and place him in irons.

SNEEP   Aye, Cap'n.

Exit sailor Sneep and pirate Harry.

MCGOVERN   So Captain Freely – It would appear your legendary treasure chest really does exist. 'Enter this chest, if you dare. In the dark find treasure rare.' Signed, 'Master Jim Watts'. Unfortunately it does not appear to belong to you, Captain Freely. I trust you can hear me? *(Silence – he draws his sword.)* Captain Freely? *(Silence.)* Will you come out – with your hands raised or shall this chest be your coffin? I shall count to three – one – two – three. *(He puts his sword into the chest, as in a magician's trick. He does this three times, then cautiously raises the lid. It's empty. He puts his head inside.)* Captain Freely! *(His voice echoes deeply as if the box is a huge cavern.)* CAPTAIN FREELY?

He looks about him then gets into the chest. Enter Sailor Sneep – he stops short when he sees Captain McGovern standing in the chest.

SNEEP   Excuse me sir – Captain. The pirate ship, the *Horizon* is escaping out to sea.

MCGOVERN   Then go after them – and be swift about it.

SNEEP   Aye, Cap'n – and shall we – will you – I mean – be joining us?

MCGOVERN   Obey the rules sailor – rule number one.

SNEEP   Never question the captain, Captain.

MCGOVERN   Then do as I command.

SNEEP   Yes Captain. I mean aye Captain.

MCGOVERN   And tell the surgeon to give you a patch for that eye.

SNEEP   Thank you Captain – and – *(Exit.)*

They salute each other and Sneep exits.

With as much dignity as he can now muster, Captain McGovern closes the lid of the chest.

Music.

ACT ONE, SCENE TWO
Kidnapped

Present day: The walls of a modern room now close in around the chest and thus we are transported to the bedroom of Jim Watts, an eight year old boy whose obsession with all things piratical is reflected in it. On the floor appear two 'toy' ships although they are in fact excellent replicas, model ships – that appear to be sailing across the bedroom floor. These ships, one a small pirate sloop and the other an English man-o'-war, are Jim's prize possessions. Jim enters in his pyjamas. He is clearly upset and before closing the bedroom door he shouts downstairs –

JIM   I hate you – and her. I hate everybody – and I'm not going tomorrow – I don't care if I promised. *(He shuts his door. He sits on the side of his bed and fumes – then he gets up again and opens the door and shouts –)* They are stupid and ugly and mean and nasty and you can't make me see them – not if I don't want to. And I don't want to – ever – *(He shuts his door sits on the side of the bed then gets up opens the door and shouts)* – And I'm not hungry anyway. *(Jim lies down between the two ships and makes battle sounds, imagining that he is hit by musket fire. Eventually he stops and burrows his head in his hands. He gets up and opens the door, but now his tone is softer.)* Why do they have to come at all? Stupid ugly twins – Why can't she just come here – alone? That's what I agreed to, that's what she agreed to and now she's gone and broken it. She breaks everything. *(Silence.)* I know you can hear me. You can tell her I don't want to see her. I'm locking the door now – and I won't open it – not for you or her – I hate you – both! *(He locks the door and put the key back in a small* box. *Seeing his mother's letters, he takes a handful of them and throws them down on the floor.)* And I never want her to write to me again.

Jim has two toy sharks and in play fashion he makes the sharks eat and fight over the letters. Behind him Captain Freely opens the chest lid and sees him. She looks around and then silently gets out of it – and draws her sword.

FREELY   Don't move – don't make a sound or you'll be deader than a dead man.

JIM   Dad?

FREELY   If it's death you want laddy – this blade is willing to oblige. If its life you're after – turn around – slowly. *(Jim turns and gasps.)* And don't start squealing – you hear me? Now answer my questions straight and true – understand? *(Jim nods.)*Is your name – Jim Watts? *(Jim nods.)* Pleased to meet 'ee Jim. What place is this? Answer me!

JIM   My bedroom.

FREELY   How very strange. Very strange indeed. *(She picks up a telescope and examines it.)* Yours?

JIM   Who are you? What are you?

FREELY *(pocketing the telescope)* What do I look like? Eh?

JIM   A – a pirate.

FREELY   Aye – a very bad one – that is to say a very good – bad one. Now then Jim, let's to the core of the apple, to the very pips of it. Where's my treasure?

JIM   Treasure?

FREELY   There it was you see – and suddenly – it was gone – and where's it gone, hey Jim? Where? Here perhaps – in your – bedroom.

Suddenly the door handle moves. We don't see Dad, only hear his voice.

DAD   Jim – you okay?

FREELY   If he comes in – you'll be the first to fall.

DAD   Jim?

FREELY   Answer him – nice and easy.

DAD   We can talk all this through you know – Jim are you listening?

JIM   Yes.

DAD   And you shouldn't lock the door – I told you before – it's dangerous.

JIM   I'm okay – I'm just – playing.

DAD   What's the point of having rules if you don't obey them? Will you open the door?

JIM   I can't open the door.

DAD   Jim – this is not funny. Open the door. On the count of three – one, two –

JIM   I can't.

DAD   Why not?

JIM   Because –

FREELY   Careful.

JIM   There's a pirate in my bedroom.

Captain Freely puts her blade to his throat.

DAD   I see – a pirate?

JIM   A very bad one. *(Captain Freely shakes her head.)* A very good – bad one – and she'll –

FREELY *(mouths)* Run me through.

JIM   Run me through – if you come in.

DAD   Okay Jim – okay. Well *(Pause)* 'Jim lad' – I suggest – you disarm this pirate – and you run him through.

JIM   It's a woman.

DAD *(sighs)*   Whatever – just run the pirate through – if that's what you need to do – and then we'll sort things out – about tomorrow. But I won't have you talking to me like you did just now. You understand me Jim?

JIM   Yes. I'm sorry –

Phone rings off-stage.

DAD   That'll be your mother – I'll tell her you'll stick to the arrangements – yes?

Captain Freely senses he is about to say 'no' and mouths 'YES'.

JIM   Yes.

DAD   That's better – Don't forget to brush your teeth.

They listen to Dad's footsteps fade – and the phone stops as he answers.

FREELY   Brush yer teeth? What on earth for?

JIM   To be clean.

FREELY   What a very odd idea. Now then, where have you hidden it?

JIM   Hidden what?

FREELY   Me doubloons, me pieces of eight – the gold, boy – the gold. Everything that was in that chest.

JIM   I don't know what you're talking about, or how you got into my house – but I do know that you are in serious trouble.

FREELY   Oh? Who with?

JIM   W – W – W – with me.

FREELY *(grabs him)* With you?

JIM   And my dad, and the police, anyone in a uniform.

With a yell Captain McGovern now leaps from the chest. Jim yells too and tries to escape the savage sword fight that now takes place in his bedroom. He tries to open the door – but it is locked of course.

JIM   Dad! Dad!

Captain Freely grabs him again, covering his mouth.

MCGOVERN   Let the boy go.

FREELY   Boy's mine captain!

MCGOVERN   Our troubles are nothing to do with him.

FREELY   Then what's his name doing – carved on my chest?

MCGOVERN   You see lad, what kind of person we have here – all she cares about is her precious gold – gold that never belonged to her in the first place.

FREELY   You have no idea Captain McGovern, what I care about – or what kind of person I am.

MCGOVERN   The kind who takes children hostage – threatening their lives, just to save her own skin.

FREELY   Seeing as you care so much for children Captain – perhaps you should lower your sword and step away from the chest. *(To Jim)* Get in.

JIM   Get in?

FREELY   In the chest – now.

JIM   What for?

FREELY   For to see what we shall see lad – before I lose my temper – big time!

MCGOVERN   Do as she says. Her threats are real enough – she has no feelings that you or I would recognise as human – or womanly.

FREELY   Don't cross me Captain.

MCGOVERN   Cross you? I will see you hang Captain Freely – for the pirate you are.

JIM   Sir?

FREELY   Shut up – and put yer head down. Down!

MCGOVERN   Don't worry lad – I will follow you both to the ends of the world if I have to.

FREELY (*looks at the room*) I think you've already done so Captain, and whatever this world is – it ain't ours.

She closes the lid. Silence. He approaches the chest opens it – with his sword raised but they have gone. He looks around the strange room – and at the ships. On them he sees and examines two small figurines – a pirate and a naval Captain. Bemused he replaces them. He sees among the letters a striking one with a red royal seal upon it. He breaks the seal and reads it swiftly with a grim countenance.

MCGOVERN   'In this the year of our Lord 1718 – I the one Sovereign King of England do hereby grant all pirates – A free and open Pardon. Lay down your weapons, give up the ways of piracy – and the King's forgiveness will be thine – forever.'

No, no I'll not have it. There'll be no forgiveness for you Captain Freely. I will see you hanging from the yard arm of my ship before that day dawns.

He puts the letter in his jacket and then approaches the chest – and he gets in. Music. He closes the lid and as it closes the lights fade and the walls of the bedroom vanish in the same way that they appeared.

ACT ONE, SCENE THREE

On the *Horizon*

Sneep the pirate drags a wet-looking Harry on to the deck of the pirate ship. Of the two miniature ships only the pirate one remains.

SNEEP   Harry, Harry. (*Sneep slaps Harry, and then pumps his chest. Harry coughs and regains consciousness.*) Harry –

sweet pirate. I thought for a terrible moment the sea had stolen you and that I was all alone in the world. From this day forth I will never let anything – or anyone come between us. It's you and me against the world – Oh Harry. *(He hugs Harry.)* But tell me, how did you escape the English navy?

HARRY   They were going to give me fifty lashes Sneep – fifty lashes across me back.

SNEEP   Certain death.

HARRY   That's what I reckoned, so I played dumb – like I was really, really stupid.

SNEEP   ...Difficult.

HARRY   And when they thought I had no thought to escape I made a run and jump for it, straight into the sea. They fired muskets at me, Sneep!

SNEEP   The devils.

HARRY   But I dived down and down into the deep cold darkness. I thought I was a dead one – next thing I knew, I saw a light above me – and then I was staring up at your face – like an angel you seemed Sneep – an angel.

SNEEP   Oh Harry.

They embrace.

HARRY   Where's the Captain?

SNEEP   Harry – you're looking at him.

HARRY   Hey?

SNEEP   Captain Freely's gone. We'll never see her again.

HARRY   Gone?

SNEEP   Forever.

HARRY   Captain Freely – gone – forever?

SNEEP Don't douse yer cheeks on her behalf Harry. She'd shed no tears over you. A heart of stone that one. So I have taken command of the ship. 'Captain Sneep' – Sounds good don't it?

HARRY *(unsure)* Yes.

As Sneep talks, the treasure chest once again appears behind him.

SNEEP I'm going to be the most infamous pirate captain that ever flew the black flag. Captain Kidd they'll say? Black Bart, Flynn, Silver – Sparrow? They were all nothing when compared to Captain Sneep of the *Horizon*. And you know what it means, don't you Harry?

HARRY *(nods)* No.

SNEEP It means that you are second-in-command. Think of it my friend – you've always dreamed of coming second.

HARRY Yes – yes – but if the captain got in the chest – what if she comes out again?

SNEEP Hey?

HARRY The chest you see – it's there – here – again.

Sneep looks slowly round, sees it and then looks back at Harry.

SNEEP Still there?

HARRY Out of nowhere. *(Sneep draws his sword and turns on the chest.)* Don't go no closer Sneep – that chest can swallow a pirate whole.

Sneep approaches – music as he opens the lid.

SNEEP It's empty – I am Captain still.

Jim leaps up from inside the chest.

JIM Agh!

HARRY/SNEEP Agh!

HARRY It's alright Sneep – it's just a boy.

SNEEP   A boy?

HARRY   A boy – wearing – something strange.

SNEEP   Who are ya? What are you doing in there? Get out – out. *(Jim gets out of the chest.)* Shall I run him through Harry?

HARRY   What for?

SNEEP   For giving me a fright – jumping up like that – all strange and unsuspected.

HARRY   I tell you Sneep – that chest is cursed – cursed – cursed.

Captain Freely calmly arises from the chest.

FREELY   Don't overdo the cursing Harry.

HARRY   It's Captain Freely. It's Captain Freely.

FREELY   Sneep! Take yer filthy mitts off the boy or I'll have your kidneys for supper. Go nicely with a pickled eye.

HARRY   You see who it is?

SNEEP   Yes – Harry.

FREELY   What's the trouble, Sneep, ain't ya pleased to see me?

HARRY   He thought you dead and gone and made himself captain in your place.

SNEEP   Thank you – Harry.

FREELY   Ha, ha! Praise be, the chest has brought us home Jim. Home to my very own ship, and my very own, scheming, back-stabbing, treacherous little gang of pirates.

She tweaks their cheeks.

HARRY/SNEEP   Ow! Who's he?

HARRY   And what's he wearing?

FREELY   This my boys – is the key to our future happiness – as in 'wealth' – one rather frightened Jim Watts.

HARRY/SNEEP   Oh?

FREELY   Wearing something called – Jim Jams – so he tells me.

JIM   Where am I?

FREELY   You're at sea, lad.

JIM   You stay away from me.

HARRY   OOOOH.

JIM   I order you I command you, to take me home. NOW.

SNEEP   Got some edges on him this one Cap'n.

HARRY   In his 'Jim Jams'.

JIM   I'm not frightened of you. I'm not frightened at all. I'm – I'm – I'm –

He starts to breathe rapidly as if about to have a panic attack.

FREELY   Relax Jim. These lads will do you no harm. Give yourself a moment here – to find your sea legs. Breathe deeply, slowly. That's good salt air, clean and fresh as any Monday. And that rocking motion – why that be the big blue – the great giver and taker itself – the sea.

JIM   No – it's not true, it's not true.

HARRY/SNEEP   'It's not true, it's not true.'

FREELY   You mind yer tongues – unless you want to see em on a plate next to yer eyes and kidneys. *(She gives Jim back the 'spyglass' telescope she took from his room.)* He's in a strange place with strange people, and must be made welcome.

JIM   No, no you don't understand. I must get home.

FREELY   Home? A pirate ship is all the home a boy could ever dream of.

JIM   But I can't be here. Wherever here is – I can't. Because – I have to meet my mother – tomorrow – I made a promise. *(Harry laughs.)* Why's he laughing?

FREELY   Harry is a happy sort Jim – he means no harm. *(Harry laughs.)* Why he laughs is a mystery – even to himself – but he's brave enough and will laugh like a hound in the face of death. *(Harry laughs again.)*

JIM   Well stop it, I don't like it. I don't like any of you at all – and I never will.

Silence.

FREELY   But we'll not take offence at that, will we lads?

SNEEP   Course not Cap'n, no offence at all.

FREELY   This is Sneep.

JIM   Sneep?

FREELY *(in Jim's ear)* Mean, greedy and vicious – never believe a word he says.

SNEEP   Pleased to meet 'ee Jim – I'll be looking after your safety –

FREELY   And Harry – you have met.

HARRY   Handsome Harry – is me full name.

Harry shakes hands with Jim.

FREELY *(in Jim's ear)* Loyal, kind, trusting and completely stupid.

HARRY   Welcome aboard –

FREELY/HARRY/SNEEP   The *Horizon*!

SNEEP   Captain! Sail ahoy!

FREELY   Spyglass. Jim? SPYGLASS!

Jim gives her his telescope. The replica English naval ship enters.

SNEEP   What is she, Captain?

FREELY   HMS *Vengeance.*

SNEEP   Again?

FREELY   Presumably without her Captain.

HARRY   How do 'ee presume that?

FREELY   Because the chest is here – not there.

HARRY *(bemused)* Oh right.

JIM   But what do you want with me – how – why am I here?

FREELY   You my boy, are here for the sole purpose of having an adventure, with me on the open sea. The second sole purpose is to unravel the secrets of this chest and help us find our treasure.

SNEEP   What shall we do Cap'n?

FREELY   'Tis nearly night, dim our lights and if fortune favours us we'll be out of sight by morning. If not –

HARRY   We'll have a great big battle, hey Jim!

FREELY   Don't scare the lad, Harry.

HARRY   He ain't frightened Cap'n – he said so three times.

FREELY   Yes – be as watchful as you are dull Harry and stand guard over this chest. If Captain McGovern pokes his head out, cut it off and shut the lid.

HARRY   Aye Captain.

FREELY   Jim – come to my cabin – Sneep – take the first watch. As in now!

SNEEP   Aye, Cap'n – *(Aside to Captain Freely)* but tell me that when you have discovered the secret of that chest – I won't have to share my gold with no boy – in Jim Jams.

FREELY *(draws a knife on Sneep)* Get aloft Sneep and be happy about it. What, do I not hear you singing – are you not a happy crew?

HARRY/SNEEP   Oh this is a jolly life we lead upon the seven seas,
Searching for a pot of gold wherever it may be.
As we sail we sing along, we sing most happily,
Cos we are free to spend our days, searching endlessly.
Yo – ho – ho – searching endlessly.

We'll down our grog and spend our tin
Freely go on a freshening wind
Searching endlessly
We'll wake all night and sleep all day
There ain't no rules that we obey –
Searching endlessly.
Cos that's the way we love to live
A lot of take and not much give
Yo – ho – ho – searching endlessly.

ACT ONE, SCENE FOUR

The Captain's Cabin

Harry and Sneep remain visible during this scene. Harry guarding the chest, and Sneep above, on watch.

FREELY   So Jim – last but not least – I am Captain Freely. This 'ere's my ship – the *Horizon* and this is my cabin – cosy hey?

Jim grabs a knife.

JIM   You take me home – now – I mean it...

FREELY   That's a sharp blade Jim, but you're welcome to have it.

JIM   Have it?

FREELY	Yours – a gift.
JIM	But I'm not allowed knives.
FREELY	Not allowed?
JIM	Of course not, they're dangerous.
FREELY	I should hope so too – and if you cut yourself it's your own fault.

Silence – he lowers the knife. He examines the cabin.

JIM	What year is this?
FREELY	Year?
JIM	What's the date?
FREELY	Not sure – exactly. Does it matter?
JIM	Yes!
FREELY	Well then – it's the year of our lord – seventeen eighteen.
JIM	1718?
FREELY	And in 1718 – Jim Jams are not in fashion.
JIM	1718. I know that date.
FREELY	You can't go around dressed like that, not if you want to be one of us.
JIM	But I'm not one of you, I'm Jim Watts, and I'm –
FREELY	A touch confused. 'Tis only natural. But I say – live for the moment Jim. Go with the wind. You are here – so – you might as well enjoy yourself. I stole these from a Spanish gentleman, hence the fancy buckle – try 'em on, lest you want Harry to laugh at you all day. *(Jim begins to dress as a pirate.)* And to keep the sun off your head, a wide brimmed hat, with a feather in it. Now don't that make you feel better. And of course every pirate must have one of these.
JIM	A real cutlass?
FREELY	To defend oneself if attacked. *(Grins)* When.

Jim thrusts the weapon forward.

FREELY   No, no, it's a slashing, hacking weapon – very good when the fighting gets up close and nasty.

Jim slashes and hacks the air.

FREELY   There you go, now all you have to do is learn – the pirate yell.

JIM   The pirate yell?

FREELY   Yes, because we like to avoid real fighting if we can– it tends to hurt. So we simply try to terrify folk into dropping their weapons and giving us their money. But you have to yell like you mean it, or they won't believe you – so – *(Captain Freely does the pirate yell.)* Now you try. *(Jim yells.)* Together. *(They both yell.)* Excellent. *(Captain Freely starts to lay the table – instinctively Jim sits up. He is given food.)* Now yer one of the crew – a pirate – so lets get down to pirate business. The chest. How did you come to own it – so to speak?

JIM   I don't know – it just –

FREELY   Appeared?

JIM   In my bedroom.

FREELY   When – if you don't mind me asking?

JIM   I think – Mum and Dad bought it together – before – and they gave it to me, for toys and things.

FREELY   About four years ago perhaps?

JIM   Yes, perhaps.

FREELY   Which is the same amount of time – I've been missing it – as it chances.

JIM   That chest – is my only way home – isn't it?

FREELY *(shrugs)* You've only just arrived Jim, why talk of leaving? We need time, don't we, to get to know each other. You like me well enough I hope. Cos I like you Jim, indeed I do. Why not stay a while – have some fun?

JIM   I told you – I have to be home – by eleven o'clock tomorrow morning – I made a promise.

FREELY   What's a promise to a pirate? We make 'em and we break 'em.

JIM   But I haven't seen her –

FREELY   Who?

JIM   My mother.

FREELY   You haven't seen yer mother?

JIM   For four years.

Silence.

FREELY   And why is that Jim?

JIM   She – left.

FREELY   What, an' never came back?

JIM   She travelled a lot – but she wrote all the time – I've got hundreds of letters – from far away lands – and places like that. Hundreds.

FREELY   Can you read then?

JIM   Of course – I've read some of them so often I know them off by heart.

FREELY   Very nice. Very impressive.

Jim slashes the air with his cutlass.

JIM   And tomorrow I have to see her – and her children.

FREELY   Her children – did you say?

JIM   Twins – by another man. I've never met them. I don't want to meet them.

Jim slashes the air more aggressively.

FREELY   Want to slice 'em all up, hey Jim, into little bits?

JIM   A million tiny bits Captain, bits so small, no one can see them – or come to their rescue – ever.

FREELY   There's a picture. *(Jim sits.)* Tired yourself out Jim? Have some grog.

JIM   Grog?

FREELY   Rum. You know – Rum – help you sleep.

JIM   I'm eight years old Captain – I can't drink alcohol.

FREELY   Oh? Still – you sit there and rest a bit.

She gives him a blanket. As she does so Sneep and Harry start to hum the tune of the song above – and it becomes a kind of lullaby.

JIM   I am tired Captain, tired right through – to the very core of me – to the very pips.

FREELY   You learn swiftly Jim – very swift indeed.

JIM *(dreamily)* Tell me Captain – about the chest.

FREELY   Oh – there's a bedtime yarn if ever I told one. *(The Captain lights an oil lamp – by which light she will tell the story. During the story she drinks grog.)* That chest Jim, has special qualities, as we have both discovered. I first heard of it from an ancient mariner who spoke of a 'magic' treasure chest. If you find it you have to empty it, quick as you can and then shut the lid – you open the lid again – and lo and behold the chest is full of gold 'again'. Imagine that. That kind of treasure chest – you only have to find once – obviously. Now I had that chest for four years, and we were never poor in those days cos the chest kept refilling itself. But then – one dark day – I lost it in a grim and bloody sea battle, with a certain Captain James McGovern – whom you have met, in passing. I had a different ship then – but he sank it – and the chest went floating away. It was awful to see it floating off Jim – awful – my treasure – my future. However, I escaped from the Captain, and have been searching for that treasure chest ever since – until yesterday, as it chances, when it washed up on Fortune Isle.

JIM *(sleepily)*   Fortune Isle.

FREELY   Aye Jim – and here's the mystery – when we opened that chest – the second time – the gold had disappeared completely. Gone. And there was something else – the chest had your name upon it – and some other mysterious words.

'Enter this chest, if you dare. In the dark find treasure rare.' So that's what I did Jim – I got in the chest – but I didn't find my gold – did I? I found – *(Jim snores.)* Aye Jim – you sleep – tomorrow will be a long day.

Captain Freely takes another swig of grog and falls instantly to sleep, as do the other pirates. Jim's sleep is fitful and the sound of the sea, the creaking of the boat, lends the action a dreamlike atmosphere, in which we hear now the music of 'The Chest'. Slowly the chest fades from view. Sneep the pirate becomes once again, Sneep the sailor – wearing his blue naval coat – and an eye patch – but on the other eye. He takes up an identical sleeping position on the other side of the stage, which now becomes the deck of the Vengeance. Darkness falls.

ACT ONE, SCENE FIVE
Battle Stations

Lights rise. Dawn. The chest now appears on the deck of the Vengeance and from it emerges Captain McGovern. As he does so the dreamlike atmosphere fades.

MCGOVERN   Get up you lazy heathen – up – up – up.

SNEEP   Cap'n?

MCGOVERN   Asleep on the watch, hey sailor?

SNEEP   Captain McGovern!

MCGOVERN   That's twenty lashes.

SNEEP   Where have you been, Captain? – And how did you get on board?

MCGOVERN   Rule number one.

SNEEP   Never question the captain, Captain.

MCGOVERN   Where's the prisoner?

SNEEP   The prisoner?

MCGOVERN   The pirate we captured on Fortune Isle.

SNEEP   He escaped.

MCGOVERN   Forty lashes! How did he escape?

SNEEP   He made a run and jump for it – straight overboard. Whether he was brave or completely stupid I cannot say – but he escaped.

MCGOVERN   Any sign of another sail?

SNEEP   No Captain, an' I have watched the waves – all night – like a hawk.

Captain McGovern takes out his own spyglass and scours the sea – until he sees – in the distance as it were – the replica pirate ship.

MCGOVERN   Like a hawk you say?

SNEEP   Aye, Cap'n – like a hawk – and a buzzard – and an eagle – and other birds – of that nature – with keen eyesight. *(McGovern hands Sneep the spyglass, and the eagle-eyed Sneep looks through it. Silence.)* Captain –

MCGOVERN   Yes, sailor?

SNEEP   I must report – there is pirate ship half a mile off the larboard bow.

MCGOVERN   Yes indeed – sailor – a pirate ship. There – just there!

SNEEP   Fifty lashes should do it captain.

MCGOVERN   Fifty? – I should lash you from here to kingdom come for the danger you have put us in.

SNEEP   Aye, Cap'n – I will not do so again.

MCGOVERN   Obey the rules. If you can't obey the rules, sailor – you might as well be a pirate! *(He looks through the spyglass.)* You're lucky, it appears they are asleep – upon that pirate ship. Perhaps we may surprise her yet. Prepare for battle.

SNEEP   PREPARE FOR BATTLE!

MCGOVERN   Quietly –

SNEEP   QUIETLY!

On board the Horizon the shouting wakes Jim with a start.

JIM   Captain – Captain – wake up – wake up.

FREELY   What is it lad?

JIM   The English navy – there – look.

FREELY   Jim lad – you have saved our skins this day – and no mistake. Harry, wake up Harry!

HARRY *(stretches)* Morning Cap'n.

FREELY   BATTLE STATIONS!

HARRY   BATTLE STATIONS!

FREELY   All hands to quarters –

MCGOVERN   And clear for action.

HARRY   Aye, Cap'n.

SNEEP   Aye, Cap'n.

FREELY/MCGOVERN   BATTLE STATIONS!

End of Act One.

ACT TWO, SCENE ONE
A Sea Battle

FREELY   BATTLE STATIONS!

HARRY   BATTLE STATIONS!

FREELY   All hands to quarters –

MCGOVERN   And clear for action.

HARRY   Aye, Cap'n.

SNEEP   Aye, Cap'n.

FREELY/MCGOVERN   BATTLE STATIONS!

JIM   The chest? It's gone.

HARRY   It ain't gone Jim – it's over there – It's on their
deck –

JIM   But how will I get home?

FREELY   No time for that –

JIM   But Captain –

FREELY   You are not the centre of attention, not here – not
now. Three points a'starboard.

HARRY   Aye Captain.

MCGOVERN   Two points a'port – steady as she goes.

SNEEP   Aye, Cap'n.

FREELY   Raise the gun ports –

MCGOVERN   And roll the guns for'ard.

HARRY/SNEEP   Aye captain.

HARRY   Come on Jim!

*Pirate Harry and Navy Sneep push on two life-sized cannon, one
for each ship.*

HARRY	Now we come to it, eh Jim, blood and guts.
JIM	Harry – we cannot win this battle.
HARRY	Who cares – it's the taking part that matters. *(Laughs.)*
MCGOVERN	Master Gunner?
SNEEP	Aye, Cap'n.
MCGOVERN	Fire a warning shot across their bows.
SNEEP	Aye, Cap'n.
JIM	Captain – that is a – a fourth rate, ship of the line – with forty guns – at least!
FREELY	Know yer ships do 'ee Jim?
MCGOVERN	On my command –
JIM	And what are we? A sloop with no more than twenty!
MCGOVERN	Fire!

An explosion as Sneep's cannon recoils. Jim, Harry and Captain Freely watch the cannon ball fly overhead. A tremendous splash is heard.

JIM	You see – we'll be blown out of the water.
FREELY	Just a warning shot Jim, giving us a chance to surrender.
JIM	Then – perhaps we should.
FREELY	Are the guns primed Harry?
HARRY	Aye, Cap'n.
FREELY	Fire on my command – but not before – not before.
HARRY	Look how she comes by. *(Laughs.)* What do 'ee think now Jim, is this the life or ain't it?
JIM	Captain – she is bigger, stronger and more powerful.

FREELY   And we are lighter, quicker and more cunning. Get up the main mast now Jim. Now.

HARRY   They're coming by Captain – all gun ports open –

FREELY   Raise the white flag Jim – and be quick about it.

JIM   The white flag?

FREELY   Aye – like you say Jim – 'tis time we surrendered. Ha ha.

HARRY   Ha ha? *(Shrugs.)*

FREELY   Quickly lad – or you'll be flying that flag in paradise.

Jim raises the white flag.

SNEEP   Captain!

MCGOVERN   Yes, sailor?

SNEEP   They've raised the white flag.

MCGOVERN   I see it – curse them all for cowards. Prepare to heave to.

SNEEP   Permission to speak, Captain?

MCGOVERN   Granted.

SNEEP   They are pirates, and most likely this is some kind of trick.

MCGOVERN *(sighs)* Most likely, but I am bound by the rules of combat, and will not fire on a white flag. Pull back the guns to show them we have seen it.

SNEEP   Aye, Cap'n.

HARRY   They're rolling back their guns, Captain.

FREELY   Then we have worked a chance.

MCGOVERN   Bring us within hailing distance please.

SNEEP   Aye, Cap'n – within hailing distance please!

FREELY   Stand by Jim. Harry – make sure we're rising in the water and then fire into her rigging. When her sails are down we make a run for it – understood?

HARRY   Aye, Cap'n.

JIM   But it's not right Cap'n – it's not fair.

FREELY   Not fair you say – forty guns against twenty – now on my word you raise the black flag – is that fair enough for ya? The black flag Jim.

HARRY   Cos you're one of us – now aren't you lad!

FREELY   Do it Jim – unless you want to see us all hanged at execution dock.

JIM   Aye Captain.

The two ships now come alongside. Both captains have loudhailers.

MCGOVERN   Captain Freely.

FREELY   Captain McGovern. Lovely weather for it.

MCGOVERN   You have raised the white flag – prepare your ship to be boarded.

FREELY   Can we not come to some financial agreement Captain – perhaps we can buy our freedom? I see you have on board a certain chest – that is worth something wouldn't you say?

MCGOVERN   I don't make deals with pirates. You are the scum of the earth and will either die in battle or at the end of a rope. 'Tis no matter to me.

FREELY   You see Jim – that's the choice he gives us – death or death.

MCGOVERN   Throw down your weapons and lower your sails.

FREELY   Now Jim – raise the black flag.

Jim raises the black flag.

SNEEP   Captain – the black flag – they've tricked us!

FREELY   Roll the guns for'ard.

HARRY   Aye, Cap'n.

FREELY   Fire – Harry – Fire.

A huge explosion sends Captain McGovern and Sneep sprawling.

FREELY   Ha ha.

JIM   Ha, ha.

HARRY   Ha, ha, ha. Oh?

FREELY   Harry – their sails are still intact.

Sneep and Captain McGovern are in a Nelson and Hardy–like pose.

MCGOVERN   What's the damage to our ship?

SNEEP   Our sails are full of holes but still working.

HARRY   If we can't outrun her – we'll have to fight it out –
with cutlasses. Argh!

JIM   Argh!

SNEEP   She'll try to outrun us Cap'n but we'll still catch her
easily enough.

FREELY   Unless there's another way to slow her down.

HARRY   You tell us how Cap'n – we'll follow you to the end
of the world, won't us Jim?

JIM   Aye – to the end of the world.

FREELY   I believe you Jim. Bring out the plank Harry – make
it nice and visible.

HARRY   Aye, Cap'n.

JIM   The plank? But who is it for Captain?

FREELY   – You, Jim. You.

JIM   Me?

FREELY Don't take it personal lad. Put a blindfold on him Harry.

JIM But why? What have I done?

FREELY Do it Harry!

JIM Get off me.

HARRY You have to do as the Captain says Jim. You just have to –

SNEEP You should see this Captain McGovern.

MCGOVERN What is she doing?

SNEEP Another trick I dare say – they have brought out the plank.

FREELY Now don't you worry, Captain McGovern thinks himself a decent man, and he will have no choice – but to stop and save you.

HARRY *(getting the idea)* Oh – Oh.

FREELY If I thought they'd stop for Harry I'd throw him overboard instead – but he'd let him drown. He won't let you drown – I know that much about him so be a good lad and stay in the water as long as you can, while we escape.

JIM But Captain –

HARRY They're watching us sure enough, Captain.

JIM You asked me to stay with you –

FREELY And you asked to go home – and the only way I know is through that chest – which is on board that ship – not this one. You see Jim, everything I do, is for your own good – even – putting you in the water – it's for your own good.

JIM Harry?

Harry laughs falsely.

FREELY Don't take it bad Jim – when it comes down to it – you don't want to be like me. I know it – you know it.

JIM   I hate you. I hate you!

FREELY   I know that an' all – I hate myself sometimes Jim –
but I'm a survivor – and so are you. So just keep breathing – nice
and easy – don't panic now – just keep breathing –

HARRY   Jim lad!

*The plank is withdrawn and Jim falls. The moment he does,
everything slows down. Music, as Jim enters the water. Exit Captain
Freely and Harry taking with them – the deck of the Horizon.*

ACT TWO, SCENE TWO
Boy Overboard

*Jim flounders and sinks deeper into his fears. We hear the sound
of his breathing, first in panic then slowing down. Watery music
accompanies a large number of envelopes, addressed to him, which
start to float dreamily by. He tries to grab them but cannot. It is
this commotion that attracts a shark. Eventually there is just one
envelope left. The shark approaches.*

SHARK ONE   Well, well – what have we here? Looks to me like
you're in some kind of trouble – some kind of – predicament.
Would that be true? Oh – after this are you? Come on then –
come on.

*The shark grabs the letter just as Jim was about to get it. Another
shark enters.*

SHARK TWO   Will you stop that – stop it at once. Give it back now.

SHARK ONE   What?

SHARK TWO   The letter.

SHARK ONE   What letter?

SHARK TWO   The one in your jaws – obviously. Give it. Give it.

SHARK ONE   I was just mucking about – if he doesn't want to muck about – what's he doing down here?

SHARK TWO   He's come for his letter – obviously. 'Jim' I assume?

SHARK ONE   Jim?

SHARK TWO   Jim Watts – that's his name. Says so here.

SHARK ONE   Oh – hey Jim *(As if talking to a foreigner)* – you've got a letter. Why doesn't he say something?

SHARK TWO   Because he's drowning – obviously. A boy out of air.

SHARK ONE   Painful. Perhaps I should put him out of his misery.

SHARK TWO   You leave him alone.

SHARK ONE   They say they taste better without the wrapping.

SHARK TWO   You take one sniff – one bite and I'll – I'll –

SHARK ONE   Alright! Who's it from?

SHARK TWO   His mother.

SHARK ONE   Nice – wish I had one – to write me a letter.

SHARK TWO   Ssh! This isn't about you.

SHARK ONE   It never is, it never is.

SHARK TWO   'Dear Jim, I'm sorry it's been so long since my last letter, but time seems to fly by when you're on the road. I know I haven't seen you for a long time, and I'm sorry for that, more than you can know – so let's break the ice Jim, and start over. Of course – if you don't want to I'd understand. You might not like our kind of life – it's a bit chaotic. I know your father runs a 'tight ship' at home, and I suppose he's had to. On the other hand you might like the change of pace – and the freedom – there'd be plenty of time for us to talk – and get to know each other again – there's so much for me to tell you – and explain.'

SHARK ONE   Goes on a bit doesn't she?

SHARK TWO   Shh. 'Perhaps you'd like to spend a weekend with us in our new Volks – wagen – camp – er – van.

SHARK ONE   What's that?

SHARK TWO   Don't know – sounds long though. 'I've been telling the twins all about you, and I was wondering if it was time we all got together, the four of us. I'd understand – if you are still angry with me, and don't want to do this. I know that what I did was wrong – in most people's eyes – and maybe it was – but I need time Jim – now I'm older – and you're older – to tell you why I left. Why I had to be free.'

SHARK ONE   Blah blah blah. Look – there's someone coming.

SHARK TWO   But I haven't finished the letter –

SHARK ONE   I can scare 'em off if you want. One bite will do the trick.

SHARK TWO   You stay back – I think they've come to save him.

The sailors pull Jim to the surface.

SHARK TWO   Do you think he'll be alright?

SHARK ONE   The thing is – do I really care? I mean, do you?

SHARK TWO   Obviously.

SHARK ONE   But didn't you want to just – eat the three of them. Really quickly and noisily.

SHARK TWO   No.

SHARK ONE   But you're a shark.

SHARK TWO   Obviously – and yet it seems we don't have much in common!

SHARK ONE   Obviously.

Exit sharks in opposite directions, obviously.

ACT TWO, SCENE THREE

An English Man-o'-War

Harry and Sneep pull Jim onto the deck of the Vengeance.

MCGOVERN   Is he alive?

SNEEP   Only just, Captain.

MCGOVERN   Tie him tight and call me when he comes to his senses.

HARRY/SNEEP   Aye, Cap'n.

They make Jim secure.

SNEEP   Wake up, lad.

HARRY   Wake up!

Jim coughs up some water and opens his eyes.

SNEEP   There you are – welcome – Jim.

JIM   What are you doing? Why am I–? Sneep? Harry?

HARRY   Hey?

JIM   It's me Jim. What are you doing in those uniforms?

SNEEP   These?

JIM   They belong to the English navy.

SNEEP   And so do we.

HARRY   We was born in these jackets lad – feels like.

JIM   I don't understand. What ship am I on?

HARRY   His Majesty's ship.

SNEEP   HMS *Vengeance*.

JIM   But I – I – I – *(He starts to breathe rapidly.)*

SNEEP   What's he doing?

HARRY   Hold it together lad, breathe nice and easy – nice and easy.

JIM   I fell into the sea, I was sinking, deeper and deeper – and there were fish –

HARRY   Fish you say?

SNEEP   They weren't fish – they were sharks.

JIM   They read me a letter.

Silence.

SNEEP   Say that again...?

JIM   They read me a letter – from my mother.

Harry and Sneep laugh.

HARRY   Or is that possible?

SNEEP   Don't be stupid.

JIM   It was strange, I was frightened at first – but then it was like I was – I was –

SNEEP   Drowning? Your life flashing before your eyes?

HARRY   That's when we pulled you out.

SNEEP   Saved your miserable skin.

JIM   But where's Captain Freely?

SNEEP   Captain Freely sailed off, and we couldn't catch her because we had to stop and save you – you little pest.

HARRY   Be nice to him Sneep – hey – for me.

JIM   Why am I tied up?

HARRY   Because – you are a prisoner.

JIM   Why?

HARRY   Because – um –

SNEEP   You're a pirate!

HARRY   That's the one.

JIM   But listen to me – both of you. You are pirates too.

HARRY/SNEEP   How dare you!

SNEEP   Say –

HARRY   Such –

SNEEP   A –

HARRY   Thing.

SNEEP   It was a pirate – looked a bit like Harry – poked my eye out. I hate pirates. We are English sailors.

HARRY   Always have been.

SNEEP   Always will be.

JIM   I – I am very confused.

HARRY   I can see that – Sharks reading letters. Huh – really.

JIM   But I must tell you, there are two pirates on Captain Freely's ship, who are exactly like you, in shape, voice and character. Everything except the blue coats.

HARRY   I don't like that – that's spooky that is.

SNEEP   Now you listen to me – Jim lad. You've had a brush with death and it's done your head in.

JIM   Only the patch Sneep, is on the other eye, on the other ship.

HARRY   Very spooky.

SNEEP   Don't listen to him – it's just a trick to unsettle us. They're full of tricks, these pirates. Call the Captain, he'll sort this one out.

HARRY   Captain McGovern!

The captain approaches, as he does so Harry takes out a whistle and pipes the captain on deck. The sailors salute.

SNEEP   Captain on deck.

MCGOVERN   So, Jim Watts. Look at you now.

JIM   Captain?

MCGOVERN   I am disappointed in you, Jim.

JIM   I'm not a pirate.

MCGOVERN   You're dressed as one.

JIM   I had no choice.

MCGOVERN   No? I've heard grown men say much the same. Seen good sailors turn pirate, tempted to lead what they think will be a 'free' life, free from responsibility and routine. Why, it wouldn't surprise me if there were two men just like these on board that pirate ship.

JIM   There are Captain.

MCGOVERN   Exactly – and one day they will end up in chains, awaiting punishment, as you are now.

JIM   But I'm not a pirate!

MCGOVERN   I saw you raising the pirate flag – and laughing as you did so.

JIM   But – I – I...

MCGOVERN   Had no choice? *(Jim bows his head.)* Perhaps I should not be angry. I understand you see – a boy might easily be tempted to the pirate way. Never wishing to do a day's work always thinking to get rich quick – off the backs of others. Freedom she may call it, I call it something else, and one day I will see that woman hang for her crimes.

JIM   But why, why do you hate her so much?

MCGOVERN   Because she thinks she can do exactly as she pleases. Rob and steal, and then sail away leaving others crying in her wake, to deal with the consequences of her selfishness.

JIM   But Captain – surely, she doesn't deserve to die?

MCGOVERN   How can you look me in the eye and say such a thing? She took you in, made you feel at home and when it suited her, she abandoned you. Made you walk the plank, just so she could escape.

JIM   But, it was for me – for my own good. That's what she said.

HARRY   What's he doing?

SNEEP   He's crying.

HARRY   What, real tears?

MCGOVERN   Release the boy. Release him!

Harry and Sneep release him.

MCGOVERN   Forgive me Jim. Her faults are not yours – I see that, and it is only just that I offer you a second chance. Fetch the boy a jacket.

SNEEP   A jacket, Captain?

MCGOVERN   Rule number one?

SNEEP   Never question the captain, Captain. Why can't I remember that?

MCGOVERN   We lead a strict life here, Jim. We do our chores, we sleep, we rise, we eat, we work and through it all, we follow the rules. This wooden world is our home; these men, are my family. Your second chance is this – join us – be one of us. Join the navy. *(He offers the coat – Jim steps forward.)* But remember – there's no going back. Join me and my crew – and you become a pirate-hater.

After a few moments Jim puts on the jacket.

HARRY   There you go Jim.

SNEEP   Bah!

MCGOVERN   Now dry your tears, there be enough salt water hereabouts. These sailors will show you the ropes and explain the rules we live by.

HARRY/SNEEP   Aye, Captain.

The Captain stands aside.

HARRY   Lovely rules they are an' all, Jim.

SNEEP   You've got to learn to do, exactly as you're told without question. That's rule number one –

HARRY   And two and three.

SNEEP   Can you do that, Jim?

HARRY   Can you follow the Captain's rules?

MCGOVERN   Put your lungs into it lads – aren't you happy in your work?

SNEEP   Rules, rules, rules, rules,

HARRY   We follow the Captain's rules.

JIM   Why are you singing?

HARRY/SNEEP   It's one of the Captain's rules

We sing when we are happy, we sing if we are not.

We sing in every weather, whether it's cold or hot.

MCGOVERN   More enthusiasm, if you please.

HARRY/SNEEP   *(louder)* Whatever he commands we're eager to obey

And if we don't agree with him, we never – ever – say.

Rules, rules, rules, rules,

We follow the Captain's rules.

SNEEP   Any questions?

JIM   Surely the captain can't be right, all the time.

HARRY   He's missing the point.

SNEEP   Entirely. The captain is always right, especially when he's wrong.

HARRY   It's – one of nature's laws.

SNEEP   How can I put it?
The sea will always taste o'salt, the wind will fill the sails
Rules like these are heavenly, they never seem to fail

HARRY   The sun it rises eastwards,
and sets down in the west
A golden rule you surely see that sailors love the best.

HARRY/SNEEP   Rules rules, rules, rules.

JIM   We follow the captain's rules.

HARRY   Now he's getting it.

SNEEP   He'll tell you when to go to bed,
and when to climb aloft.

HARRY   He'll tell you when to WAKE UP!

SNEEP   And when you can cast off.

HARRY   He'll give you grog for doing good,

SNEEP   The lash for being bad,

HARRY/SNEEP   It may seem rather simple,
but it's perfect for us lads.
Rules, rules, rules, rules,
We follow the Captain's rules.

SNEEP   And when it comes to battle,
don't ask if wrong or right
Simply do as you are told

HARRY   And then enjoy the fight.

SNEEP   It's the duty of the Captain,

HARRY   To see that we don't sink

SNEEP   The rules are there to save us

HARRY/SNEEP   Having thoughts to think.

HARRY/SNEEP/JIM   Rules, rules, rules, rules,
We follow the Captain's rules.

HARRY/SNEEP   *(in sweet harmony)* And if we didn't have them, we'd never work so well
We'd mostly fight and squabble, and then one day – rebel.
So we let the Captain rule us, awake and in our dreams
That's the way the navy is, in seventeen eighteen.

SNEEP *(grabs Jim roughly and snarls)* Understood, Jim lad?

JIM *(dreamily)* 1718, 1718.

HARRY   What's the matter with him?

JIM   Our Captain – is breaking his own rules. *(Silence, then a crack of thunder.)* What was that?

SNEEP   What do you mean, 'breaking his own rules'?

JIM   To obey the King's commands.

MCGOVERN   Stand by for rough weather, men – storm coming in.

JIM   1718 – I remember now. That's the date – the very date the King of England offered – the pirates of the Caribbean – a chance – to be forgiven.

SNEEP   What are you talking about?

HARRY   Yeah? What?

Another crack of thunder.

MCGOVERN   Trim the mainsails – fore and aft – and secure those barrels.

JIM   Let go of me Sneep and I'll explain – The King – in the year 1718 – offered the last pirates of the Caribbean – a pardon. All they have to do – is – stop being pirates and they can walk away – free. If you haven't heard of this – it means Captain McGovern has disobeyed the King and kept it secret from you.

Another crack of thunder – the ship starts to roll.

HARRY   We follow the Captain's rules Jim – didn't we sing it clear enough?

JIM   If the King wants to forgive Captain Freely, – then that's what should happen.

SNEEP   Now you look here, Jim.

JIM   No you look here – we cannot sail under a captain who disobeys the King – can we?

SNEEP   How do you know about this 'pardon'?

JIM   I read it – in a book. I've read loads of books – about pirates and sailors. We have to do something – before Captain McGovern catches her.

HARRY   Do what?

JIM   – Take over the ship. We have to force him – to give the pirates the chance the King has offered.

HARRY   But that's –

SNEEP   Mutiny!

Another crack of thunder – Captain McGovern approaches.

MCGOVERN   What are you men doing? There's a gale blowing – we must secure the ship – or sink with it. All hands to quarters – move. Move! *(They have frozen. Jim draws a cutlass. Sneep follows.)* What's this?

HARRY   Don't do it Sneep – don't do it!

MCGOVERN   Draw swords against me – would you – Jim Watts? It seems you be a pirate still.

JIM   Captain McGovern – do you have in your possession, a letter – from the King of England?

MCGOVERN   What's that you say?

HARRY   I'm no part of this Captain.

Harry draws his sword and stands with the captain.

SNEEP   If such a letter do exist Cap'n – please show it us.

JIM   Now!

MCGOVERN   You mean this letter – do 'ee Jim? With the King's seal upon it?

SNEEP   It's true then. Harry?

HARRY   I am stupid I know – but I am loyal – to the captain of this ship.

SNEEP   Farewell then Harry –

HARRY   My brother –

JIM   You must deliver that letter, Captain. It's the law.

MCGOVERN   Indeed, I will not. I will see Captain Freely hang before I see her forgiven. You have my word on it.

JIM   Why? Why do you hate her so much?

MCGOVERN   The same reason as you Jim – the same reason –

JIM *(yelling over the storm)* But I don't hate her, – I don't – hate her!

A crack of thunder again and lightning. In the storm that follows we see the four fighting. During the confusion Jim gets the letter from Captain McGovern.

HARRY   We're sinking, Captain! She's going down.

SNEEP   Harry!

HARRY   Sneep!

MCGOVERN   Abandon ship – abandon ship.

The storm reaches its climax. Silence and darkness falls.

ACT TWO, SCENE FOUR

Return to Fortune Isle

The gentle sound of waves. Captain Freely, Jim and Captain McGovern have been washed ashore and lie prostrate on Fortune Isle. Jim wakes.

JIM Captain Freely? You can't be drowned. I won't let you be. Wake up – wake up. *(Jim shakes her violently. Then he sees Captain McGovern.)* Captain McGovern?

FREELY Ahhh.

JIM Captain Freely?

FREELY Jim lad, is that you?

JIM Oh Captain – I thought you were dead.

Jim impulsively hugs her.

FREELY I thought so too lad – and in that death I had a terrible dream. I dreamt there was a storm at sea and my lovely little ship – sank beneath the warring waves.

JIM That was no dream Captain. Your ship is sunk, and so is his.

FREELY My ship. My ship. – Is he alive?

JIM I don't know–is he?

Captain Freely goes over to Captain McGovern.

FREELY Unfortunately. But see here Jim – The chest – The chest is here again. Fortune Isle – same as before – an' I can smell gold Jim. It's full this time, I can smell it – gold, gold. Gold.

JIM Is that all you care about – the gold?

FREELY No! With gold I can buy another ship. A ship means – freedom. Let's open it – together – what do you say?

Jim stands back as Captain Freely approaches the chest – music as before. She opens it. It's full of gold.

FREELY   Ha, ha, ha. – Look lad – here, take it – take as much as you want. I'm alive again. What's the matter? Jim?

JIM   I want to go home.

FREELY   Home – what for? Our adventures have only just begun. We're pirates and we're rich – rich.

JIM   You stay away from my gold.

FREELY   Yours?

JIM   Mine.

FREELY   Don't shut the lid, Jim! That's the thing see – shut the lid and the gold might vanish – like a dream.

JIM   Then keep away – it's my chest – got my name on it.

FREELY   Pull a sword on your own captain?

JIM   You're not my captain. You just appeared out of nowhere – kidnapped me, threw me in the sea – like I was nothing – all for this? And what of Harry and Sneep – you haven't given them a second thought. Captain McGovern was right about you, you don't care about anyone except yourself.

FREELY   Ow, ow, ow. Why Jim, I hardly know where I stand with you. One moment it's all hugs and kisses the next you want to run me through.

JIM   Well that's how I feel – so you be careful. I wanted to help you – but you don't deserve it.

FREELY   Deserve what – exactly?

Jim throws the pardon over to her.

FREELY   What's this?

JIM   A letter from the King of England.

FREELY   And where'd you get it?

JIM   I took it from Captain McGovern, by force. *(He jabs his sword at her.)* The King offers you a chance – to come home – read it. He will forget and forgive all your past crimes and let you live – all you have to do – is stop being a pirate.

FREELY   Me? Stop being a pirate?

JIM   You'll be free, Cap'n. Free.

FREELY   I thank 'ee kindly Jim – I do – but I can't stop being what I am – and as for freedom – I won't have that – no Jim – not at home. They'd take my ship – my sword – make me fetch and carry, cook and clean, is that the life for me, Jim?

JIM   You stay back – I'm warning you.

FREELY   Jim – I don't want – or need their forgiveness – yours perhaps – if you would give it me? You risked your life to bring me this – letter from the King. You fought for me without regard to your own safety. No one has ever shown me such care, I'm sure I don't deserve it. I know I don't and here you are still trying to help me. I can't understand why, after all I've done – but I can value it – I can – as much as any treasure. So you go ahead and shut that lid – and clear your passage home. It's morning you know. You have an appointment to keep – don't ya? Go on.

JIM   You'd give up the gold?

FREELY   The gold and the chest – so you can go home. Well – that's what you want – ain't it?

JIM   I don't believe you.

FREELY   Then step aside, and I shall prove myself.

She approaches – suddenly disarms him – and then glares at the gold takes a few coins. Behind her Captain McGovern is regaining consciousness.

FREELY   I must be blooming bonkers.

She shuts the lid. As it closes Captain McGovern attacks and they fight. The action mirrors the previous fight in Jim's bedroom.

JIM   Stop it – stop fighting – stop fighting – please – please. *(They stop – but have their swords at each other's breasts. They stare at each other.)* Just – stop it – forever and ever.

MCGOVERN   Go home Jim – go on

FREELY   You have an appointment to keep.

JIM   I will not go – until you throw down your swords – throw them down now.

FREELY   Jim lad – this is something you cannot control, cannot stop.

JIM   But you must stop one day – you'll have to – you'll just have to.

MCGOVERN   This is our fight lad – ours.

FREELY   And you are not the cause of it – so open the lid Jim.

MCGOVERN   'Tis time for you go.

Music – he opens the lid – it is now empty. He gets in and closes the lid – the captains fight.

ACT TWO, SCENE FIVE

Treasure Found

The two captains continue their fight as the walls of Jim's bedroom come up around them. They fight out through the door and thus exit. The door closes. Morning. After a few moments, Jim emerges from the chest and closes the lid.

JIM   10.45

DAD *(off)*   Jim?

JIM   Dad?

DAD *(off)* I thought I told you not to lock this door. Are you okay? Are you ready?

JIM Yes – um – no – what time is it?

DAD Time to open the door.

Jim opens the door and his Dad steps into the room. He is dressed in a modern day naval uniform.

JIM You going to work?

DAD *(nods)* An emergency meeting at the base. The fleet is on standby. So did you run that pirate through?

JIM Not exactly.

DAD Escaped?

JIM I think so.

DAD Pirates are tricky. So – you have fifteen minutes.

JIM On deck in ten, Captain.

DAD Good, I'll put breakfast out – but you'll have to hurry.

JIM Okay – Dad?

DAD Yes son? – What is it?

JIM Do you miss – do you miss – the sea? I mean if mum hadn't left – you'd be on board a ship – somewhere – wouldn't you?

DAD Probably – but um – this ship does me just fine Jim – just fine. As long as the crew do their duty. Now –

JIM Dad?

DAD Yes.

JIM It's okay for me to go – isn't it? To see mum.

DAD I don't understand.

JIM You don't mind?

DAD   Jim – of course – It's all arranged. What?

JIM   – You used to say – she could never see me.

DAD   Said a lot of things, Jim. Things I shouldn't have said. Things you shouldn't have heard.

JIM   So you – forgive her now – for leaving?

Silence – then Dad looks at his watch.

JIM   Dad?

DAD   – I can't honestly say I forgive her for hurting you. But I do understand her better now than I once did. Not easy. *(Pause.)* There's an old saying, Jim, that opposites attract. Well your mum and me are opposites, we attracted and after that we did nothing but fight.

JIM   All the time?

DAD   Not at first.

JIM   Is that when you bought the chest?

DAD *(surprised)* Yes. We bought it in – an old shop – down by the sea. I remember the day. Pretty old – huh?

JIM   Very.

DAD   The thing is Jim – your relationship with your mother is different to mine – something separate, special and at the end of the day – she's your mum – always will be – and –

JIM   And?

DAD   And if I've made that relationship difficult – in the past – then I'm sorry – truly sorry.

JIM   So it's okay then?

DAD   Yes Jim. Its okay. I want you to see your mum – I want that very much. *(A honk of a horn from the road.)* That's her.

JIM   Are the twins there?

DAD   I guess.

Jim picks up his cutlass.

JIM   She could have left them with grandma – just for one day – couldn't she?

DAD   I think so. Yes – I think so – and you can tell her.

JIM   I will.

DAD   That's the spirit. I – I know she'd like to come up and see your room – would that be alright?

JIM   Without the twins?

DAD   Yes. I can – I can keep an eye on them – while – the fleet can wait.

JIM   Okay.

DAD   You get your things together.

Exit Dad. Jim closes the chest lid. He tidies up the letters into a bundle and puts an elastic band round them. He breathes deeply in and out. The sound of the sea. His mother enters, and stands in the door way watching him. She is dressed in something, not exactly hippy – but very much the opposite of a uniform. Jim is holding the letters. He turns.

MUM   Hi Jim.

JIM   Hi mum.

Lights fade.

The end.

Production Images

Imagination Stage production of *Pirates!*

Josh Sticklin as Jim, Phillip Reid as Harry
and Colleen Delaney as Captain Freely.

Tim Getman as Captain McGovern
and Michael John Casey as Sneep.

Polka Theatre production of *Pirates!*

Tunde Makinde as Captain McGovern,
Ben Sewell as Sneep.

Rachel Nott as Captain Freely.

Cahoots NI PRESENTS

NIVELLI's War

www.cahootsni.com

WRITTEN BY CHARLES WAY
DIRECTED BY PAUL BOSCO MC ENEANEY
MUSIC BY GARTH MCCONAGHIE

Illustrator: Lee Boyd. Design by Gillian Mee.

NIVELLI'S WAR

Nivelli's War was commissioned by Cahoots Theatre, Northern Ireland and will open February 26th, 2014 at the Market Place Theatre, Armagh, Northern Ireland. A play for all over 7 years.

Director Paul Boscoe McEneany, Music Garth McCoaghie, Design Sabine Dargent.

Characters

This play is written for a minimum cast of five.

The stage manager

The Great Nivelli

Mother

Father

Ernst

Mr Dethier

Tante Sophie

Mr H

Russian soldiers (2)

The princess

Stephan, the butler

American soldiers (2)

Notes

Some of The Great Nivelli's lines are done as a recorded voice-over.

At the end of the text is a version of Scene Six in which the Russian soldiers speak Russian. It would be my preferred option for the scene to be performed in this way – but it can work with all speaking English as in the main body of the text.

SCENE ONE

A theatre.

A stage.

The stage manager walks onto the stage pushing before him a wide faced broom. How many times has he swept this stage? A large bunch of keys hangs from his belt. After a few glum sweeps he drops the broom and leaves. He returns with an easel which he places to one side. But maybe the other side would be best... No. Now he's gone again – returning with a picture/poster of this evening's act.

'The Great Nivelli' –

He places the picture on the easel and stands back to study it. The Great Nivelli wears a dark shabby coat and an old battered black hat. He wears white gloves that seem to shine with their brightness. In one white hand he holds a bunch of brightly coloured balloons which float above his head. The Great Nivelli is smiling and it really is an infectious smile because now the stage manager is smiling too. Who would have thought – such a famous magician performing on his stage? He takes from his pocket a piece of paper – and after reading it he leaves again returning with a small table – like so. It seems so little for so famous an act. Now he sweeps the stage with renewed vigour. Wait. What is that sound? He looks at his watch. Too early for the Great Nivelli, surely? A frown returns to the stage manager's face which in truth has not seen enough sunlight these past few years. That noise again. He'd better go and see. How annoying – just when he had found himself a little joy.

The Great Nivelli enters wearing a dark shabby coat and a battered black hat. He is smiling just like in the picture. When he realises no one is there the smile drops from his face. He thinks to himself.

NIVELLI *(recorded VO)* Oh – maybe I'm a little early.

He looks at his watch. Oh – It isn't on his wrist.

NIVELLI *(recorded VO)* Mm that's odd where's my –

He pats his pockets and finds the watch in his overcoat top pocket.

NIVELLI *(recorded VO)* Ah there you are.

He puts it on his wrist. He looks at his watch.

NIVELLI *(recorded VO)* I am early. Well, well, not like me.

NIVELLI   Hello – Anyone about?

Now he sees his own face on the poster.

NIVELLI *(recorded VO)* Oh there you are. Never late – not you. Always get to the theatre first don't you? Always smiling. Triumphant. Yes – I know, I know – how much younger than me you look – but you're not really. No – you just don't age between performances. What am I doing – I'm talking to a picture?

He walks away but then turns back to the picture, wagging his finger at it.

NIVELLI   You know how long this journey was? How tired I am? That would wipe the smile from your lips.

He puts the suitcase on the table. It's an old brown suitcase that has seen some miles. He gives it a pat. Now he looks around.

NIVELLI *(recorded VO)* My my – what an old theatre it is – very old – it's a miracle really. What's that?

He hears a muffled sound from somewhere in the theatre.

NIVELLI   Hello?

(recorded VO) Oh yes someone's coming now.

(To the poster) I know – I know – don't forget to smile –

The stage manager enters. The smile returns to The Great Nivelli's face.

STAGE MANAGER Oh – Mr Nivelli – you're here. You're here. I am so sorry –

NIVELLI   Yes – I came through the stage door.

STAGE MANAGER Oh and I wasn't there to – *(He looks at his watch.)*

NIVELLI   Yes – I'm a little early –

STAGE MANAGER I can't believe it – The Great Nivelli – standing there – on my stage – after all this time.

NIVELLI   Please call me Ernst.

STAGE MANAGER The Great Nivelli.

NIVELLI   Yes – it's been a few years since I – Ernst – was last here.

STAGE MANAGER We put you in all the papers – The Great Nivelli – returns to his home town. We're honoured.

NIVELLI   Thank you. Thank you.

STAGE MANAGER Overwhelmed.

NIVELLI   Thank you.

STAGE MANAGER Overjoyed.

NIVELLI   It's a lovely old theatre.

STAGE MANAGER Amazing how it survived the war.

NIVELLI   I was thinking the very same.

STAGE MANAGER   So many buildings round here were reduced to rubble.

NIVELLI   Yes – I used to live – just –

STAGE MANAGER   I have swept this floor a thousand times for some very famous actors but I have never been happier than today – sweeping it for you.

NIVELLI   Ernst.

STAGE MANAGER   The Great Nivelli.

NIVELLI   Thank you.

STAGE MANAGER   Even your poster brought a smile to my face.

NIVELLI   You're very kind. *(He scowls at the poster.)*

STAGE MANAGER   Shall I show you to your dressing room?

NIVELLI   No – I would like to stand here for a few minutes. Get the feel of the theatre. You understand.

STAGE MANAGER   Of course. I shall leave you alone. Every artist has their own routine – their own mystery.

NIVELLI   That's right.

STAGE MANAGER   But let me take your coat.

NIVELLI   Thank you – thank you

STAGE MANAGER   And your hat.

NIVELLI   And my hat too? Very well – take it.

STAGE MANAGER   Welcome Home – The Great Nivelli. *(The stage manager walks away and soon realises that he does not have the hat. He turns to see Mr Nivelli wearing it as before.)* Forgive me Mr Nivelli – I don't –

NIVELLI   Oh my – yes.

The stage manager reaches for the hat and does not see or feel the coat slip from his arm. He turns away and when he realises that he has it no longer he turns back to see the Great Nivelli wearing it as before – and smiling just as on the poster.

STAGE MANAGER I don't know what the matter is with me today – *(He returns for the coat losing the hat in the process.)* I don't know what I'm thinking. *(He loses the coat – the hat – the coat – and suddenly realises –)* OH! OH! YOU! Ha, ha – marvellous. What a privilege. To be made a proper fool of by the Great Nivelli. I shall tell my grandchildren.

He turns with the hat and coat – but realises he has lost his keys. The smile falls from his face. He takes the keys from Nivelli and marches off. From the suitcase Mr Nivelli takes out an identical hat and coat and puts it on. He looks at his watch. It's not on his wrist. He pats his pocket and as before finds it in the top pocket. He shrugs. He then takes three cups and four balls from the case and places them on the table. Next, a bottle of wine and a glass. He then takes out a white pair of gloves – puts them on exercising his hands as he does so. He does a practice trick. He hums to himself.

NIVELLI *(recorded VO)* Practice, practice, practice.

He looks at the smiling poster of himself.

NIVELLI *(recorded VO)* Yes, thank you – no, I didn't forget. I didn't –

He goes to the poster and turns it around so the smiling face is no longer visible. He is satisfied with this. He then puts everything back in the suitcase but takes out a new packet of balloons (which he nearly forgot) opens them and blows one up. At the first blow – he hears a musical sound. He looks at the balloon then blows it again and once more a musical note is heard. He stares at the balloon – then blows again and as he blows the music develops and to Mr Nivelli's surprise he sees something descending from the darkness above him. A small baby basket. He stares at it. The stage manager enters but stops short when he sees Mr Nivelli wearing the hat and coat.

STAGE MANAGER Mr Nivelli – forgive me –

NIVELLI Yes?

STAGE MANAGER Tea?

NIVELLI   Tea?

STAGE MANAGER   Would you like some?

NIVELLI   Tea lovely – Uh do you – uh? *(He points into*
the air.)*

STAGE MANAGER   Milk?

NIVELLI   Yes milk – no sugar.

STAGE MANAGER   No sugar.

NIVELLI   Do you – I mean do you–? *(He points vaguely into*
the air.)*

STAGE MANAGER   Are you alright Mr Nivelli?

NIVELLI   Yes, yes – a long journey. I just wondered if you saw
– never mind.

STAGE MANAGER   Milk, no sugar.

NIVELLI   Thank you, thank you.

The stage manager goes. Mr Nivelli is left in silence. He suddenly lets the balloon go which makes the usual funny sound and the basket goes back up. He finds the balloon and blows again. Music as before – and the basket begins its journey back down. Now it is met by a woman in a 1930's dress. She takes a baby from the basket. Very carefully Mr Nivelli ties a knot in the balloon. The woman is now joined by a young German soldier with a camera. He takes a photo. He takes the baby from the woman's arms and the woman takes a photo of the soldier and the baby. Then the soldier takes a picture of all three of them with the camera held at arm's length. As Nivelli watches this scene his hand moves to his own wallet – for in it is this actual photo. Now the soldier is kissing the baby. In the distance they hear the sound of gunfire. The soldier gives the baby back to the woman and then turns away – he goes back to kiss her – and the baby too. Now he turns and is gone. She waves. She waves.

Nivelli stares at his mother. How young she seems. How real – it's as if he could touch her. Nivelli steps towards her – but suddenly she has gone. Silence.

Nivelli returns to his suitcase and picks up another balloon. He hesitates then blows again. The sound of the gunfire returns and is joined by louder explosions – and the more he blows the balloon the louder it gets. When he finishes blowing the balloon there is silence. He feels someone watching him and turns to see a young boy. Could it really be? Yes – himself – what would he be about six years old? How ragged he looks. The boy is staring at him. What does he see? A man in a black coat and battered hat in the street – selling balloons. Nivelli holds out the balloon and the boy takes it from him – and runs home. His older self follows.

SCENE TWO

ERNST   Mama. Look I've got a balloon.

MAMA   You're late.

ERNST   I've got a balloon.

MAMA   And it's almost dark – where have you been?

ERNST   It's a balloon.

MAMA   Look at your knees –

ERNST   Fell over.

MAMA   Where?

ERNST   On my knees.

MAMA   I've told you a hundred times Ernst – a thousand times not to play in those houses. And you've cut yourself?

ERNST   It's a balloon.

MAMA   They're dangerous. Don't you understand? Full of old rusty nails and if you get one of those stuck in you – you'd get blood poisoning – and there's nothing I could do to save you because there's no medicine anywhere in the city. Hey? Look at me. And what if you trod on an unexploded bomb? BOOOM – where would you be then?

ERNST In bits.

MAMA *(she hugs him)* I like the balloon very much – of course. Who doesn't like balloons? Show me the person who doesn't like balloons and I'll eat my apron. *(She puts the apron in her mouth and growls. Now she fetches a bowl to wash his knees.)* Looks bad. Doesn't it hurt?

ERNST No. *(She applies the cloth and water.)* Ow.

MAMA Who were you playing with?

ERNST Torvald.

MAMA Just Torvald?

ERNST Torvald's going away to Furstenhagen next week. He says he doesn't know when he'll be back.

MAMA The war will be over one day Ernst. The children will all come back.

ERNST What if the war doesn't end?

MAMA It will end. I'm telling you it will. *(She blows on his knee to dry it.)*

The Great Nivelli watches.

MAMA Wash your hands. Lay the table now.

ERNST What's for supper?

MAMA Beef soup – and bread. I got the last loaf of the day. *(They sit. Ernst peers at the soup.)* What are you looking for?

ERNST Beef.

MAMA Close your eyes. Oh lord we give thanks for this beef flavoured soup – We give thanks for our great nation and pray that the war will be over soon – *(Silence)* and that Ernst's friends can come back to Frankfurt.

ERNST Amen.

MAMA Amen.

MAMA   I'll take a bowl up to grandpa – you can start if you want to.

ERNST   No – I'll wait.

Mama exits and we hear her go upstairs. The Great Nivelli watches his younger self staring at the soup. Suddenly Ernst eats the soup – it's gone. Mama returns. She sits and eats a few mouthfuls.

MAMA   Do you want some more? *(Ernst shakes his head.)* Maybe you should go upstairs then and say goodnight to grandpa.

ERNST   Do I have to?

MAMA   He can't get out of bed Ernst. He waits all day for a little visit from you. Go on. *(Ernst goes and Mama pours most of her soup into his bowl. The Great Nivelli watches her as she puts her head in her hands. She is exhausted. She puts on the radio and listens. Ernst comes down stairs. He sees there is more soup in his bowl.)* There was more in the pot – go on.

The air raid warning siren goes off. Ernst is instantly tense but Mama doesn't panic though. Mama turns off the radio and listens. She nods at Ernst to finish the soup. She gets his coat. She takes his balloon. Herr Dethier enters.

DETHIER   Ernst – stop that and get down the cellar – now. Hurry along now Frau Beckmann.

MAMA   Really Herr Dethier we are quite capable –

DETHIER   I know – I know – Hurry along now.

They go to the cellar and the Great Nivelli follows them.

MAMA   It's alright Ernst. We're safe down here – Isn't that right Herr Dethier?

DETHIER   Oh yes – safe as houses.

Mama glares at him.

DETHIER   Do you want to play cards Ernst? What do you want to play?

ERNST   Snip Snap.

DETHIER   Very well, very well. Snip Snap. The same as the last air raid – and the air raid before that – and the air raid before – in fact it's always Snip Snap, isn't it Ernst? Oh yes – we've got quite a routine going on down here.

ERNST   Mother – will you play?

MAMA   Sure.

DETHIER   I bring the cards. You bring the coffee. The Americans bring the bombs. *(Distantly the bombs fall. They all look up.)* Quite a routine. It's strange, don't you think Ernst?

ERNST   What?

DETHIER   We hear planes in the sky and we look up – but we are in the cellar and all we can see is the floor above us – but still we look up as if we could see right through it – right through the dark sky into the plane itself. So – you want to play or what?

They play cards.

ERNST   Snip Snap. I won. I won.

DETHIER   You little man – shouldn't be here to win anything.

ERNST   What do you mean?

DETHIER   Your mother knows what I mean. You should have been sent away to the country – where it's safe – months ago.

MAMA   Please don't interfere in things that don't concern you Herr Dethier.

DETHIER   They could concern me, if you saw sense. I could look after you – and the boy when the war's over. Look after all of us. *(Silence.)* Forgive me Frau Beckmann – it's just that – we will all need someone. I will need someone – in the years ahead.

MAMA   That is true Herr Dethier – but it will not be me.

DETHIER   Why not?

MAMA   You want me to tell you – honestly – with my son sitting right there listening to every word?

ERNST   What are you talking about?

DETHIER   Your mother doesn't like me Ernst.

MAMA   That isn't true, Herr Dethier.

ERNST   Yes it is.

MAMA   Ernst.

ERNST   You told me you didn't like him.

MAMA   Oh!

DETHIER   It doesn't matter. I prefer honesty – and I honestly say to you – with respect Frau Beckmann that you should send your son out of the city – because if our soldiers are told to defend it to the death then the Americans will have no choice but to bomb and to bomb and blow up every building in every street. Who will survive it? You? Me? Ernst?

Mama pulls Ernst away and gets him ready for bed.

ERNST   Is that true Mama? Mama?

MAMA   Shh. You want this blanket too? You remember your Tante Sophie? *(Ernst nods.)* We went to stay with her at the farm – her and Rudi. Of course Rudi's not there anymore.

ERNST   She had a chicken with one leg.

MAMA   That's right – she did.

ERNST   But it could still lay eggs.

MAMA   Yes –

ERNST   But it couldn't run.

MAMA   Ernst – if the bombing gets worse – I would like you to go and stay with Tante Sophie.

ERNST   You'd come too.

MAMA   How can I go anywhere with your Grandfather in bed – unable to move? Who would feed him?

ERNST   Then I don't want to go. I won't go. Not without you.

MAMA   It isn't safe here –

ERNST   But you said it would be safe. You said you would never send me away like the other children. You promised me.

MAMA   Things have changed. Herr Dethier is right.

ERNST   I won't go – I won't go. I won't go.

DETHIER   Ernst. How dare you raise your voice to your mother.

MAMA   Please – Herr Dethier –

ERNST   I won't go. I won't go. I won't –

The sound of the planes and bombing suddenly increases. They all look up and an explosion. When the smoke clears Ernst is dressed ready to leave. His mother brings a suit case. Mama tries to smile. Ernst cannot smile. She gives him a cake. They walk to the station.

MAMA   It's a cake – for Tante Sophie. Don't eat it on the train will you? *(He hears the sound of the train and looks at his mother.)* It won't be long Ernst – I promise – and you'll love the countryside – you did before. Now look at me. Look. If you ever get lost – or anything happens – I have sewn a letter into the lining of your coat. The letter says who you are – and where you live. It's sewn in here. Ernst?

He nods his head but cannot hear.

She hugs him. He does not hug her. He scowls. The sound of the train gets louder and louder and his mother gets smaller and smaller and is gone. The Great Nivelli watches his younger self and as he fully inhabits the memory of his youthful loneliness he begins to fade from view until only Ernst remains – as the train leaves Frankfurt.

SCENE THREE

The train arrives and Ernst gets down onto the platform. The train leaves again. Ernst stares across at the only woman on the platform. Tante Sophie is a farmer's wife.

ERNST   Tante Sophie?

SOPHIE   You've not grown as much as I'd expected Ernst. Well – come if you're coming. Ernst?

ERNST   I want to go home.

SOPHIE   That is not polite. *(The boy lowers his head.)* It's not as if you haven't stayed with me before. Is it? *(He shakes his head.)* We can't stand here all day waiting for it to rain. We have a long walk ahead of us.

ERNST   Last time we went on a cart – pulled by a horse wearing glasses.

SOPHIE   Blinkers –

ERNST   It had steam coming out of its nose.

SOPHIE   I'll have steam coming out of my ears if you don't come along.

ERNST   But where's the horse?

SOPHIE   'In a better place' – that's what they say isn't it? Come – I'll carry your bag – if that's what you're wanting.

ERNST   No – I can carry it.

SOPHIE   Good. Come along then. *(Ernst arrives at the farm. A table and chair marks the interior with a ladder going up to a raised platform. The exterior is Tante Sophie's garden. He looks around.)* You remember now? The house – the garden. Sit.

He sits. She gives him a glass of juice.

ERNST   Do you still have that chicken?

SOPHIE   What chicken?

ERNST   With one leg.

Sophie stares at him.

SOPHIE   Are you making fun of me Ernst? *(He shakes his head. On the table are some flowers. He reaches for them.)* They're not real. But they don't fade – So – how is your mother? *(He offers her the cake.)* What's this?

ERNST   A cake.

SOPHIE   That city sister has learnt how to bake a cake?

ERNST   It's rhubarb cake.

SOPHIE   We have rhubarb in the garden – but don't eat it raw. It will give you diarrhoea.

ERNST   There's a note on top.

SOPHIE   Just a note? *(Sophie reads the note.)* She says a bomb fell near the house.

ERNST   Right outside. It made a big hole called a crater just by our front door and all our windows blew in and Granddad's face got all nasty cuts on it but they're better now and some bricks fell down on Herr Dethier's leg and broke it and Mama said if we'd been in the kitchen none of us would have got out of there alive.

Silence.

SOPHIE   She always did like to exaggerate. You can sleep up there.

ERNST   Up there?

SOPHIE   I can't have you under my feet every hour of the day and night – can I? Go. *(He climbs up – and she sits at the kitchen table as if exhausted by him. Ernst puts down his bag.)* Bombs – we don't have. What we have is foxes.

ERNST   Foxes? *(He is drawn to the window and looks out as if to see foxes.)*

SOPHIE   Where there are chickens there are foxes. Come in the night – stealing everything that is rightfully ours. Of course when your Uncle Rudi was here he kept them out and no mistake.

ERNST   Where is Uncle Rudi?

SOPHIE   I thought your mother would have told you that. He's in the east – in the army. I expect to hear from him any day. Any day – *(She picks up a shirt she's been mending)* – until then you're the man of the house – that's why you've been sent here Ernst to help me keep those foxes out of my garden. You can see the chicken shed quite clearly from your window, quite clearly. *(As he looks a light rises on the chicken shed.)* The chickens and the vegetables are all we've got, you and me. It's you and me against the world now –that's what they say isn't it –

She stares off into the distance – losing the train of her thoughts.

ERNST   Tante Sophie?

SOPHIE   Can you bark?

ERNST   What?

SOPHIE   Can you bark?

ERNST   You mean – like a dog?

SOPHIE   Of course like a dog. Go on – try – try for Tante Sophie. *(He barks.)* Louder. *(He barks again.)* Now if you see a fox from the window – I want you to bark – like that. If you see a fox – any type of fox coming out of the woods back there – out of the woodwork – that's what they say isn't it – you just bark – because if you don't those thieves will steal everything right from under our noses and leave us to starve. But you won't let that happen will you Ernst? Will you?

ERNST   No.

SOPHIE   That's a good boy. So – *(Again she seems lost in her own thoughts.)* Good night, Ernst.

ERNST   Goodnight Tante Sophie.

Music.

Ernst – now armed with this job stares down on the chicken shed and vegetable patch. His aunty sits downstairs and begins to work on the shirt collar with a needle and thread. She pushes the cake to one side. Ernst watches the moon rise. He listens to the sound of the night. It sounds new and wonderful. Before long Sophie falls asleep. Ernst tries to keep watch but eventually he too falls asleep. He does not see a man in a dirty coat and battered black hat sneak just like a fox into the garden. The man goes into the chicken shed, emerges with a chicken and then sneaks away. Ernst wakes to the sun in his face. When he goes downstairs Sophie is standing with the shirt in her hand staring into space. He is about to say something to her but instead creeps past into the garden. He goes into the chicken shed – and emerges holding an egg. He looks around – realising that one chicken has gone. He then stops – and stares at the ground. He runs inside.

ERNST   Tante Sophie? Tante Sophie?

SOPHIE   Who are you? What are you doing here? Why are you in my house?

ERNST   I – I'm Ernst.

SOPHIE   What – Who?

ERNST   Ernst.

SOPHIE   Ernst – yes – from Frankfurt. What is it? Why are you bothering me – at this time?

ERNST   In the garden.

SOPHIE   Yes?

ERNST   In the mud.

SOPHIE   What?

ERNST   A – a footstep. *(Sophie nods.)* A footstep – in the mud, Tante Sophie.

Sophie now goes into the garden. She walks straight to the chicken shed and sees that a chicken has been stolen. She returns to Ernst and the footstep in the mud.

SOPHIE   That's our fox alright.

ERNST   A fox?

SOPHIE   Why didn't you bark?

Sophie goes back into the house. He takes the egg to her.

ERNST   I found an egg. *(Sophie nods – but she does not smile. She does not seem to know he's there.)* Tante Sophie? I'll bark next time – I promise.

She stares at him. He goes up to the loft.

Music.

The day turns to night. Ernst goes to the window and watches the moon rise. He looks down at the garden. He listens to the sound of the night. Below him Tante Sophie is talking/crying to herself as she works on the shirt. How strange – maybe she's upset about the fox. Sophie falls asleep. Ernst tries to keep watch over the garden but eventually he too falls asleep. He does not see the man in the dirty coat and battered black hat sneak into the garden. The man goes into the chicken hut. He comes out with another chicken and sneaks away. Ernst wakes with the sun in his face. When he goes down stairs Sophie is standing with the shirt in her hand staring into space. He is about to say something to her but instead goes into the garden. He looks for footsteps – finds them and goes into the chicken hut and then runs straight back into the house to tell Tante Sophie but she looks up at him and smiles and he says nothing. He finds himself something to eat. Ernst climbs the ladder and as night falls he listens to Sophie cry a little but he's used to it now and when he catches the fox she'll stop crying he's certain of it. But Ernst falls asleep and does not see the fox-man come. The fox-man goes into the chicken shed but comes out empty handed. There are no chickens left. He goes to the vegetable patch to steal some vegetables and as he's doing this Tante Sophie has woken up. She is putting on her hat and coat. She puts the shirt in her bag and comes though the garden in the moonlight. The fox-man freezes – he is holding some rhubarb. She stares at him. He stares at her. She looks up at Ernst's window and then leaves. The fox-man looks up at the window too and then leaves. Morning comes. Ernst wakes with a start – he goes downstairs.

ERNST   Tante Sophie? Tante Sophie! *(He looks for her. He goes into the garden. She isn't there.)* Tante Sophie?

Where could she be? The weather is changing – he gets a chair and a stick and sits outside. He sits for a long time – until he falls asleep – it is night time – then day time then night time and day time. Ernst falls over into the mud. Night time. It starts to rain.

SCENE FOUR

The man Ernst thinks of as 'the fox' comes out of the woods into the garden. This time he has a slight limp. He sees Ernst asleep in the mud. He creeps around the boy and steals some more rhubarb. He stares at the boy – and makes to leave. He stops – comes back – then he walks away again – then he shrugs enormously and moans – and then returns. He prods Ernst. He prods again. Ernst wakes up.

ERNST   You.

MR H   Me?

ERNST   Tante Sophie – Tante – *(He barks. Pause.)* Stay away.

He barks again.

Silence.

MR H   Why were you sleeping in the mud?

ERNST   To catch you – and now I've caught you – and you're under arrest.

MR H   Who me?

ERNST   Yes you. Stop staring. I forbid you to stare at me –
thief – fox –

MR H   Fox?

ERNST   You fox.

MR H   Me?

ERNST   Yes you and my Tante Sophie will be back soon –
with a policeman –

MR H   A policeman?

ERNST   Two policemen – and then you'll be in trouble.

MR H   Yes – yes – foxes are always in trouble.

ERNST   Shut up – thief. Put up your hands.

MR H   Who me?

ERNST   Yes you. Up, up, up.

MR H   What for?

ERNST   I told you – you're under arrest.

MR H   Who me?

ERNST   Yes you. Stop saying that. Put them up. Put them
up – Please.

MR H   Oh – please – well in that case – so politely I say
– No.

ERNST   – No?

MR H   No. I have spent the last five years with my hands in
the air – I'm really very tired of it.

ERNST   – Tante Sophie? – Tante Sophie!

MR H   Tante Sophie? The woman. Ah. The last time I saw
your Tante Sophie was four nights ago. Maybe five.

ERNST   Five?

MR H   She was talking to a shirt.

ERNST   What do you mean?

MR H   I saw her leave – in the middle of the night – this Sophie. She saw me. At least I think she did – she stood and stared right through me – like I wasn't there. Maybe I wasn't. Any food left in the house? Hey you – I asked if there was any food in the house?

ERNST   No – because you've been stealing it all – from under our noses.

MR H   Fox has to eat too.

ERNST   We shoot foxes.

MR H   This I know. *(He indicates his limp.)*

ERNST   I hate you.

MR H   I hate you too.

ERNST   What?

MR H   Ernst.

ERNST   Who are you?

MR H   Who am I?

ERNST   How do you know my name?

MR H   That one I can answer – I heard the woman calling you Ernst. So here's the truth little Ernst – with your up, up, up! I don't think your Tante Sophie is coming back.

ERNST   You're lying.

MR H   Who me?

ERNST   She will come back. She just went into town. She wouldn't leave me. She will come back. I know she will. She must come back – she must.

Ernst breaks down in tears. He curls up in the mud and weeps.

MR H　　　　　　That's enough now. Hey – I said that's enough! So you haven't eaten for two or three days – is that right? *(Ernst nods.)* Why didn't you pull up the rhubarb – or the last beetroot? Look – you're crying all over it.

ERNST　　　　　　She told me to guard it – not eat it.

MR H　　　　　　You are an obedient boy – hey? Very obedient but there's only so long a boy can go without eating before he starts seeing things – like – like an apple perhaps – with a ruby red skin floating just before him. *(Ernst sees the apple which seems to come from nowhere. He grabs it and eats.)* Not so fast. Hey – not so fast! You know Ernst – some people say the war is over.

ERNST　　　　　　Over? How can it be over?

MR H *(shrugs)*　Maybe – a war is like having your hands in the air all the time – eventually you just get tired of it. Goodbye, Ernst.

ERNST　　　　　　Where are you going?

MR H　　　　　　I'm going back to my foxhole. And you, Ernst should go home – there's nothing here for you.

ERNST　　　　　　Wait – please wait.

MR H　　　　　　Go back to the place you lived before you came here.

ERNST　　　　　　Wait. Wait! – I'm sorry about what I said –

Mr H stares at him.

MR H　　　　　　So what? Goodbye, Ernst.

ERNST　　　　　　Stop! You will please stop –

Mr H stops.

ERNST　　　　　　I know where there is plenty of food. Lots to eat.

MR H　　　　　　Oh? Let's hear it.

ERNST　　　　　　In the city my mother is waiting for me with enough food to – 'to feed an army'.

MR H　　　　　　A whole army? You must have a big house.

ERNST	Yes, it's very big. It's enormous.
MR H	I can imagine. What city?
ERNST	Frankfurt.
MR H	Frankfurt am Main?
ERNST	And you should take me there.
MR H	To Frankfurt?
ERNST	Because you stole from us.
MR H	I see – I see – but – I don't care about that. I don't care about you Ernst – or about your big house in Frankfurt – alright?
ERNST	I hate you.
MR H	I hate you too.
ERNST	I just want to go home.
MR H	Everyone wants to go home. The roads are full of such people.
ERNST	Don't you want to go home?
MR H	– Frankfurt is two hundred kilometres – at least. There are no trains, no buses – no transport at all – except for soldiers – it's impossible.
ERNST	We could walk.
MR H	To Frankfurt?
ERNST	I won't tell my mother that you stole from us – I promise.
MR H	Oh – you are very well brought up – but I don't care what you tell your mother. *(He turns.)*
ERNST	You just can't leave me here – you can't – you just can't!
MR H	And you – don't understand, little Ernst – it would take many weeks to walk – months maybe. Look at you – you don't

look as if you've walked further than one hundred metres in your whole life.

ERNST   I hate you.

MR H   You said that twice already. I accept it.

ERNST   And I never said it before to anyone but YOU – in my whole life.

MR H   Your whole life? – Your whole life... *(He walks up and down. Ernst watches him.)* Your mother has enough food you say to feed an army? *(Ernst nods.)* You know that I know that's a big lie? *(Ernst nods.)* And you know that I don't owe you 'boy in the mud' anything – not one thing. *(Ernst nods. Mr H stands for what seems to Ernst an eternity. He walks up and down again – he stares at Ernst and shakes his head – then shrugs to himself more largely than before.)* Go into the house. Find a bag – and put everything into it that you'll need. Blankets – cups, knives fork plates – three of everything.

ERNST   Three?

MR H   What's in there?

ERNST   Old things – *(Mr H disappears momentarily and returns with a bike.)* That's Uncle Rudi's bike.

MR H   Praise be to Uncle Rudi – and all his ancestors. Go – go into the house and pack what you need – before I change my mind.

Ernst goes into the house. Music. Time passes – during which Ernst packs. Mr H has taken the bike off and there is a great deal of banging and sawing. Ernst draws a picture for Tante Sophie. The banging stops Mr H comes on with a cart he has made. It has two long handles so it can be harnessed to the person pulling by the shoulders. Mr H goes into the house – he takes off his hat and wipes his shoes. He looks at Ernst's drawing and note.

MR H   For Tante Sophie?

ERNST   Is it spelt right?

Mr H nods. He then takes a few more things including the fake flowers and some real stalks of rhubarb. They go outside. Ernst stares at the cart.

MR H   Not bad hey?

ERNST   Where's Uncle Rudi's bike?

MR H   I have no idea. You can sit up there. Like a little king you are, hey Ernst. A king in his chariot.

ERNST   Is this a chariot?

MR H   Without a doubt.

ERNST   What shall I call you?

Mr H shrugs.

ERNST   What's your name?

MR H   My name. He wants me to take him to Frankfurt – and he wants my name. Well I will take you to Frankfurt – If I can. Why? I have no idea – but my name – that you cannot have.

ERNST   Why not? *(Mr H shrugs.)* What shall I call you then?

MR H   Pick a letter – any letter.

ERNST   H.

MR H   Herr H – no – Mr H.

ERNST   Mr H?

MR H   I've been called worse. Alright – say goodbye to the house.

SCENE FIVE

Music.

Soon the farm is far behind. Ernst walks beside the cart until he gets too tired, then he sits on top and watches the war-torn world pass by – images that he will remember all his life for these two are just two among many travellers. Mr H does not meet the gaze of others but Ernst looks and Ernst sees; here a wounded soldier begging, here an old couple with a small coffin, here a pregnant woman walking, here a child playing without smiling with a doll in the dirt, here a man who smiles then tries to steal something from the cart. As the journey continues Ernst feels a growing sense of danger. When a plane passes over head they cower at the side of the cart but it is only some leaflets being dropped. Ernst picks one or two up. Sometimes Mr H and Ernst walk through the night under the light of a clear moon. Sometimes they walk with others – sometimes alone. Now they walk alone. Ernst is falling asleep as he walks.

MR H   Look – Look –

ERNST   A river?

MR H   And a river may mean?

ERNST   Fresh water.

MR H *(looks around carefully)* That's right – that's right. Trees too and trees may mean?

ERNST   Shelter.

MR H   Can you see anyone down there?

ERNST   No.

MR H   Are you sure? Ernst? Ernst? *(Ernst has fallen back to sleep. Mr H grumbles and pulls the cart round to the river by the trees.)* We'll make camp here. Well – you will make camp as I have shown you. Ernst! Wake up. It's your turn to make camp.

ERNST   What?

MR H   Wake up. *(Ernst sleeps.)* Sleep then. After all – you must be exhausted pulling that cart across country all day.

He puts a blanket over the boy. Music as Ernst drifts in and out of sleep. Vague shapes drift through the air in front of him and the camp magically takes shape. A tarpaulin stretched between poles becomes a tent – lit from within by an oil lamp. A fire bursts into life and a fish finds its own way on to the flames and cooks itself. The stars shine down. Ernst wakes – he is shivering. He gazes in wonder at the camp.

ERNST　　　Fish.

MR H　　　Trout.

They eat.

ERNST　　　This is a good place isn't it, Mr H?

MR H　　　It will do.

ERNST　　　No one can see the fire from the road.

MR H　　　Which is important.

ERNST　　　And there are still leaves on the trees.

MR H　　　Which is a miracle. Sit nearer.

Ernst looks around the camp.

ERNST　　　Mr H – how long did you live in the woods, Mr H? *(Mr H shrugs.)* What did you do all day – in the woods? *(Mr H shrugs.)* What did you do before you lived – in the woods?

MR H　　　Eat your supper Ernst.

ERNST　　　Why don't you talk?

Mr H shrugs.

ERNST　　　I can shrug too.

MR H　　　No I don't think so. At least you can't shrug properly – I mean with any precision.

ERNST　　　I can shrug.

MR H　　　Well yes – not bad for a beginner but you must realise that there is more than one shrug in the dictionary Ernst.

ERNST　　　What do you mean?

MR H   Well – say you came to me with a big idea. Like – uh – 'Mr H – Mr H I'm going to live on the moon'. Then I might shrug – like so – and that may mean?

ERNST   I don't know.

MR H   A small shrug may mean – Alright, not a bad idea Ernst. Go and live on the moon if you want. Whereas a slightly bigger shrug may mean – Mm I'm not sure now about that idea – the moon – I mean really? An even bigger shrug – What? Are you crazy – you want to go live on the moon – have you lost your senses? And then you have the biggest shrug of all. *(He shrugs hugely.)*

ERNST   What does that one mean?

MR H   Go! Go to the moon – be all alone – see if I care. I wash my hands of the whole idea – in fact I never liked the idea in the first place which was the true meaning of the first little shrug but you didn't want to see it that way. Go on go – leave me – I'm not hurt – not a bit. *(Ernst smiles.)* So – those are the four basic shrugs and four will get you through childhood. Try them on. *(Ernst shakes his head.)* One, two, three, four. Try them – see if they fit. *(Ernst does the four shrugs.)* Yes – yes – very good. Though I must warn you there are plenty of other shrugs to master. Hundreds. Thousands – Millions. Now go to bed.

ERNST   I'm not tired.

MR H   No, because you slept all day – while I pulled you around like you were Alexander the Great. Now it's my turn to sleep. Finally.

Mr H gets beneath a blanket. Silence. Mr H starts to nod off.

ERNST   Would you like to see a picture of my mother Mr H? *(Mr H snores loudly.)* Mr H would you like to see a picture of my mother and me?

Mr H stares at Ernst and gives a little shrug. Ernst smiles – gives him the photo.

MR H   Oh yes – which one are you?

ERNST   I'm the baby. That's Mama.

Silence. Mr H stares at the picture.

MR H   And the soldier?

ERNST   Papa.

Silence.

MR H   Is Papa still alive?

Ernst shakes his head.

ERNST   Do you have a picture like this Mr H?

MR H   Not any more. Keep it safe Ernst. Now I'm going to sleep if I can – it's proving rather difficult.

ERNST   Do you want me to sing to you?

MR H   What?

ERNST   Mother used to sing to me – to help me sleep.

MR H   No. Don't sing Ernst – please. Keep watch if you want – bark like you used to for Tante Sophie.

ERNST   I wonder where Tante Sophie is? You think she was crazy?

MR H   I think she was upset.

ERNST   Upset about what?

MR H   The same thing everyone else is upset about – the war – everything. I need to sleep now.

ERNST   Goodnight Mr H.

Ernst practices his shrugs and then sleeps.

SCENE SIX

Early morning. It is misty and when Ernst opens his eyes he is not sure what he is seeing. Now he freezes because the shapes become real – two Russian soldiers with rifles raised walking through the mist toward them. One of the soldiers sees that Ernst is staring at him and softly indicates for him to be silent. The other soldier stands behind Mr H who is sleeping.

SOLDIER ONE   Up, up, up, up.

Ernst watches Mr H get to his feet. He looks quite comical as he searches for his hat – knocking things over as he tries to improve his appearance for these unwelcome visitors. Mr H pulls Ernst to him.

SOLDIER ONE   Who are you? What are you doing?

MR H   Don't shoot – don't shoot.

SOLDIER ONE   Who are you? What are you doing down here?

MR H   We don't understand – Hello Hello – um – we don't understand.

SOLDIER ONE   Don't talk. Don't talk.

MR H   It's alright Ernst – it's –

SOLDIER ONE   Don't talk – don't talk. Kneel. Kneel. Down, down.

MR H   I promise you it's alright. Ow.

SOLDIER ONE   Be quiet. What's all this stuff? Keep your hands up, up, up. Hey – what's in the cart – what's in the bags? Weapons, guns, grenades? Boom, boom, boom.

MR H   No. No boom, boom. No.

SOLDIER ONE   Open, open, open. No you – you – boy. Open. Now.

MR H   Go on Ernst – Go on. Open the suitcase.

SOLDIER ONE   Slowly – slowly. (*Ernst opens the suitcase and steps away as indicated by Soldier Two who then steps forward*

*and peers into the suitcase – then pulls out some clothes – roughly
throwing things about.)* What is it?

SOLDIER TWO   Nothing – rubbish.

SOLDIER ONE   Look in the cart

SOLDIER TWO   You look in the cart.

SOLDIER ONE   No you look in the cart.

SOLDIER TWO   No you look in the cart.

SOLDIER ONE   You.

SOLDIER TWO   YOU!

MR H   Wait – me – I look in the cart.

SOLDIER ONE   Stay down stay down. Stay down.

SOLDIER TWO   You German?

MR H   Yes. I German. Boy German. You Russian. Trees
– wooden.

ERNST   This Russian.

Ernst is holding the leaflet. He holds it out to Soldier Two.

SOLDIER ONE   Careful. Careful.

SOLDIER TWO   It's a piece of paper. Are you scared of a piece
of paper?

SOLDIER ONE   Depends what it says. What does it say?

SOLDIER TWO   I can't read – you know I can't read. Why do you
always want to rub it in?

MR H   It says – 'The Russians are friends of the
German people.'

SOLDIER ONE   What's he say?

SOLDIER TWO   How I should I know? Blah. Blah. Blah.

*Soldier Two crumples up the paper and throws it down at Mr H's
feet who goes to pick it up.*

SOLDIER ONE　Leave it – leave – you back – back.

MR H　　　　Oh I was just – Oh?

To Ernst's surprise where there was a piece of paper is now the bunch of flowers.

SOLDIER ONE　Hey?

SOLDIER TWO　Hah!

Mr H offers them the flowers and performs another trick.

SOLDIER TWO　Hah, hah. Do you see that?

SOLDIER ONE　Yes – I saw. Be careful though.

SOLDIER TWO　Don't tell me you're scared of a bunch of flowers. Look – Again, again. *(He holds up the gun – to make Mr H do more tricks.)* Again. Again. *(He slowly lowers the gun.)*

Mr H approaches the contents of the suitcase – and from out of nowhere starts to perform tricks by sleight of hand. Soon the soldiers drop their guns and are laughing like children. During this time Mr H relieves Soldier One of a pair of binoculars.

MR H　　　　Ernst – for this one I need your help. Come, come.

They perform another trick.

BOTH SOLDIERS　Again. Again.

SOLDIER ONE　Okay we go now.

SOLDIER TWO　Nice boy – I have a brother back home your age. You want?

He gives Ernst a drink of vodka. Ernst spits it out. They laugh.

SOLDIER ONE　Vodka. We have to go now. Goodbye. Good luck. Wunderbar.

MR H　　　　Wunderbar. Wunderbar. Goodbye – goodbye – Hey for you – friends.

He gives them some raw rhubarb – which the soldier bites into. The soldiers have gone. Silence. Mr H sighs deeply – he is shaking.

ERNST	He'll get diarrhoea.
MR H	Serve him right. Up, up, up – always the same – up, up, up.
ERNST	How did you do that?
MR H	You alright? You weren't frightened?
ERNST	I want to know how to do it too.
MR H	What this?
ERNST	Yes – that. I can't do it.
MR H	Of course you can't; it takes years of practice. We shouldn't stay here Ernst – we must move west as fast as we can.
ERNST	But I can't see how –
MR H	Come on – pack up the camp. Quickly.
ERNST	Will you show me?
MR H	Not now, Ernst, move!
ERNST	But you'll show me! Won't you Mr H?
MR H	Yes, yes – now hurry. Where there are two soldiers there's a whole army. We keep to the side roads today Ernst and go fast.

Music. Ernst and Mr H travel again. Ernst is too busy trying to perfect the trick Mr H showed him to notice that Mr H's limp is getting worse. They stop – and Mr H shows him where he's going wrong. As he does so a wind picks up – brown leaves fall and they stop and cover up as best they can. Time passes on the road. Finally Ernst masters the trick.

ERNST	I've got it. I've got it.
MR H	Shh.
ERNST	But Mr H I – What is it ?

MR H   A big house.

ERNST   A very big house.

MR H   Bigger than yours?

Ernst nods seriously. Mr H looks around as before.

ERNST   Look at the trees Mr H– like soldiers.

MR H   They're part of this estate. All this land – these trees belong to that house.

ERNST   Maybe it's empty.

MR H   Maybe it isn't.

ERNST   Maybe it is.

MR H   Maybe it isn't.

He gives Ernst the binoculars. Ernst stares at them then at Mr H who shrugs.

ERNST   The windows are boarded up.

MR H   Which may mean?

ERNST   It will be dark inside.

MR H   Which may mean?

ERNST   There's no one there. No one would live in the dark, would they?

MR H   Maybe –

ERNST   Maybe not.

The wind blows across them again.

MR H   It would be warm in there – fireplaces.

ERNST   There might be some food too.

MR H   Alright – but be careful Ernst – we sneak up.

ERNST   Like foxes.

MR H   Naturally.

Both exit, pulling the cart.

SCENE SEVEN

Ernst and Mr H now approach the back of the house. There is a large window which has been boarded up. There are long curtains too. The sound of splintering wood can be heard as they take a few boards off to peer in.

Ernst is small enough to squeeze through and is standing in the big room. He looks up and – a chandelier descends. A long table now comes across the stage. A fireplace appears. Each item materialising as he sees them. He is awestruck.

MR H   Psst. Ernst. Ernst. *(Ernst lets Mr H in. They take in the scene. Ernst is about to speak but Mr H stops him. Mr H mimes pouring a drink and drinking like an aristocrat. Ernst feels the softness of the seats. Mr H warms his backside by the empty grate and straightens his invisible cravat. Then Mr H sees Ernst staring at something – a pair of slippers by the fire. Mr H picks them up and examines them. He is concerned now. Now they look at each other in shock because from another distant part of the big house comes the sound of a piano. Mr H hides behind the big curtain.)* Ernst. Ernst.

Ernst cannot hear Mr H's voice. He is frozen to the spot. Mr H is about to go and get him when they both hear someone coming. Mr H hides.

Ernst watches as a man dressed entirely in black enters – in his socks. He goes to the fire and looks for his slippers. The piano music continues. His slippers are not there. He turns and sees Ernst. They stare at each other. Then Ernst watches the man leave the room. He looks over at the curtain – where is Mr H? Then he hears the piano music stop. Ernst listens to sharp footsteps approaching louder and louder until in a blaze of light a vision enters the room – a woman wearing a beautiful shawl over a beautiful dress and holding an oil lamp.

PRINCESS   Who are you? What are you doing in my house? Answer me.

ERNST   I was cold.

PRINCESS   Cold? Do you think that gives you the right to break into someone's house? *(Ernst nods.)* No. It does not give you the right to break into someone else's house. Under no circumstances does one break into someone else's house especially when there is a perfectly usable doorbell. *(She stares at him a long time.)* What is your name?

ERNST   Ernst.

PRINCESS   Ernst? You look – are you lost? *(Ernst shakes his head.)* No?

ERNST   I'm going home. My mother is waiting for me.

PRINCESS   Where is home?

ERNST   Frankfurt.

PRINCESS   You're walking?

ERNST   Everyone's walking – because all the trains are broken – or only for soldiers.

PRINCESS   Have you seen soldiers? *(Ernst nods.)* What kind of soldiers?

ERNST   Russians.

The princess and the butler look at each other.

PRINCESS   When?

ERNST   Two, three weeks ago. I can't remember. Are you a princess?

PRINCESS   Stephan fetch the boy a slice of bread and some ham. Stephan!

Stephan turns to go.

ERNST Please – can my friend have some too?

Stephan stops and the princess takes a step back. She nods at Stephan who searches the room. He pulls the curtain back but Mr H is not there.

PRINCESS Where is this friend? Or is he of the 'invisible' variety?

ERNST *(Shakes his head)* He's behind the curtain. *(Stephan goes back to the curtain. This time Mr H is there smiling and holding out the slippers which he puts into the butler's hand. He then bows before the princess kissing her hand.)* There's no need to be frightened – this is Mr H. *(Mr H throws back his head and laughs silently then stands next to Ernst. Mr H Smiles inanely.)* He's – he's quite harmless. Honestly.

PRINCESS Why – you just can't – you just can't! – Doesn't he speak?

Mr H shakes his head.

ERNST Well – only when he has to.

MR H *(mouths to Ernst)* – It's a long story.

ERNST It's a long story.

PRINCESS Is he your father?

ERNST No.

PRINCESS Who is he then?

ERNST Mr H – is – is helping me get home. It's – it's his job – he's getting paid. A lot. *(Mr H looks at Ernst rather surprised but then nods.)* And he's hungry –like me.

PRINCESS That may be so Ernst – but every other day some poor soul stops by this house and asks for food – as if we had a never-ending supply – and if they're not given food they try and steal it.

ERNST Is that why you boarded up the windows?

PRINCESS   Now we are forced to live like this – like bats.

ERNST   We thought there was no one here.

Silence. Mr H indicates that they will go.

PRINCESS   No – for heaven's sake. A child and a scarecrow – what do you take me for? Stop! Stephan – tonight – we have guests. Yes – that's right – guests.

ERNST   Doesn't he talk either?

PRINCESS   Only when he has to – and that I assure you is also a very long story. Please sit. Now let's brighten this place up a bit.

Ernst is now in another world – a world of flickering warmth. Music. Stephan brings food and they fall upon it like animals and laugh suddenly with their mouths full. They apologise and laugh again – then eat slowly. The princess looks beautiful to Ernst and the stern butler rather funny. The food is soon finished and they mutter humble thanks. A feeling of sorrow flows through Ernst's veins and he lays his head on his arm. If only his mother could have shared this food, this light, these faces, this palace. How he misses her. He feels a hand on the back of his head gently stroke his hair – it's the princess. The princess whispers to the butler who then leaves returning a moment later with an old packet of balloons. He presents these to Ernst and Ernst is acutely aware of the pristine white gloves the butler is now wearing. Ernst blows up a balloon and this is followed by a small round of applause which makes Ernst smile and the princess smiles too – although to Ernst there is always something sad about her. Now Mr H whispers in his ear and Ernst nods. Yes, they should do something in return for the food. Yes, Ernst will be the magician's assistant. Mr H indicates that the butler's gloves would be handy – of course the butler doesn't want to give them up but after a curt nod from the princess he accedes. Together Ernst and Mr H perform a few magic tricks for the princess and the butler who watch with increasing joy as…

1 – A bottle of wine appears inside the balloon.

2 – They see a glass floating in the air, and then

3 – A needle passes through the balloon which bursts.

All this is greeted with applause and exclamations of disbelief – even the butler is smiling. They understand now that Mr H is a conjuror – or used to be before the war. Mr H is handing back the white gloves but the butler refuses them and makes of them a gift to Mr H. Now a feeling of great tiredness comes over Ernst again – but not of sorrow just pure exhaustion and to his vision things begin to lose their solidity. He hardly feels the blanket laid over him.

SCENE EIGHT

When Ernst comes to consciousness he is once again on the back of the cart and Mr H is in the harness pulling him along on the never-ending road. It's as if the palace, the princess, and the butler were all a dream. It begins to snow. Now Mr H stops – he can no longer pull the cart – his leg is hurting too much. It is Ernst's turn to pull it and this he does with Mr H limping alongside. As they walk the landscape changes and now there is a wall – or at least what's left of a wall. And there are two soldiers – Americans, chatting easily at some distance from them. They guard one of the bridges into the city and barely give them any attention. Mr H stumbles and falls – he sits now with his back against the wall.

ERNST   Mr H. Mr H – We're here – we're here. Frankfurt. We made it. Mr H?

MR H   That's good Ernst. Go and ask them for a cigarette will you.

ERNST   Americans?

MR H   The war's over Ernst. Go on.

Ernst approaches the Americans and with sign language makes his meaning clear. At first they refuse – then we see Ernst do a small sleight of hand trick for them. He returns with a cigarette. He puts it into Mr H's mouth.

ERNST   Are you alright?

MR H   I'll be fine. You go and – you go.

ERNST   Me?

MR H   Ask those Americans if you can cross that very excellent home-made bridge of theirs. Praise them up. You know how to do it.

ERNST   But you will come too.

MR H   Later, later. I need to rest here.

ERNST   Here? But the city is just there.

MR H   I can't walk anymore.

ERNST   But Mr H – you have to come. You have to.

MR H *(sternly)* For pity's sake – I got you here – now go and find your mother. Ernst – please.

ERNST   But – I want you to meet her – I want you to.

MR H   Look – I can't walk another step – I've gone as far as I need to.

ERNST   I don't understand.

MR H   Will you please go! Go!

ERNST   But what if she's not there Mr H? What if something's happened – what if – you know?

MR H   Then come back – I'll be here. I can't walk any further. Go on!

ERNST   Is it because you still hate me?

Silence.

MR H   Before you find your mother – I should tell you something Ernst –

ERNST   What?

MR H   I used to have a little shop not far from here. We sold – cards – dice – wands – top hats – gloves – everything one would need to be a magician.

ERNST   I don't remember it.

MR H   It was before you were born – Nivelli's magic shop.

ERNST   Nivelli? That's your name?

MR H   Not my real name, Ernst – a stage name. A magician's name.

ERNST   What's your real name?

MR H   Levin.

ERNST   Levin.

MR H   Not a good name to have back then – a Jewish name. You understand, Ernst. *(Ernst nods once.)* Ernst – If you can't find your mother – come back. I'll be here – by the cart. I will rest – scrounge some food, some medicine perhaps from those Americans.

ERNST   But you can't stay here – It's so cold.

MR H   Cold? *(He shrugs enormously.)*

ERNST   And – the city looks so different Mr H. I don't – I don't recognise anything – everything's changed – gone –

MR H   You know your own address don't you? *(Ernst shakes his head.)* The name of your street – the number of your house? *(Ernst shakes his head.)* No? I brought you all this way and you don't know even know where you live?

ERNST   I know where I live –

MR H   But you don't.

ERNST   I do, I do – I just don't know what it's called!

Silence.

MR H   I tell you Ernst – I don't have a shrug big enough for this situation. *(Silence.)* Give me your coat. Give it.

He rummages through – feels the envelope – tears the stitches.

ERNST   What are you doing?

He takes out the envelope – Ernst remembers now and snatches it.

ERNST   How did you know?

MR H   Even I had a mother, Ernst. *(He takes the letter gently back.)* Egelbacher Strasse 2. Sound familiar?

ERNST   Yes. Yes.

MR H   So – ask around – that's where you live. Shoo. Shoo.

Music.

Ernst approaches the Americans – shows them the address and asks them to go across the bridge. They let him through. Mr H slumps against the wall. The Americans don't even see him. Snow falls. Ernst returns. How could he leave Mr H in that condition? The Americans treat him like a lost pal. Want him to do more tricks – but he runs past them. He stops and stares. Is Mr H dead? He shakes him – but he won't wake up. He runs back to the Americans but now they refuse to listen. He runs back to the cart and finds the binoculars and takes them to the Americans. They like this – a pair of authentic Russian binoculars. The Americans come over now and pay attention to Mr H. They have medicine. They clean and wrap his leg – make him swallow some more medicine. Ernst makes a decision and smashes up the cart to make a crutch for Mr H. With the crutch Mr H can now walk in to the city. Ernst – runs back to get the suitcase his mother left behind. The cart is left behind – for firewood for the Americans.

SCENE NINE

Ernst and Mr H stand in a street. A woman passes with a wheel barrow load of bricks – then a man passes with another load.

Everywhere people are moving bricks. A front door frame stands attached to a few of them.

MR H　　　　Do you see her? *(Ernst looks and shakes his head.)* But this is where your house – this is the right street? *(Ernst nods.)* Which house – where? *(Ernst points to the door.)* You will need a new roof Ernst – and some walls. *(Ernst suddenly sits – he can take no more.)* Hey. If she was in the cellar – or some other shelter. *(Ernst closes his ears.)* Ernst! *(Ernst shuts his eyes. Now a woman enters – she is wearing the same apron – but it's very ragged. Her hair is ragged too. It is Ernst's mother. She seems exhausted – and puts up some washing. Mr H kicks Ernst.)* Is that her? Is that your mother? *(He roughly pulls the boy up –)* Up – up – up. Look!

He pushes the boy forward. This catches his mother's eye and she turns. At first she does not believe it – but now she is running toward Ernst and now she is embracing him. A light rises now on the man Ernst will become – The Great Nivelli, who watches his younger self and his mother embrace. Now she is taking Ernst inside the house. Now the door is closing. The Great Nivelli watches Mr H leave. Now Ernst is coming out of the door.

ERNST　　　　Mr H. Mr H. Mr H? Where are you? Mr H? Mr H?

SCENE TEN

A theatre.

A stage.

The Great Nivelli – is lost in his own memories and as the vision fades before his eyes the stage manager enters with a mug of tea.

STAGE MANAGER　Tea – no sugar.

NIVELLI　　　　Where are you? Where are you?

STAGE MANAGER What's that?

NIVELLI I never saw him again you see – he disappeared.

STAGE MANAGER Who?

NIVELLI The man who taught me my first magic trick – when I was a boy. I was just – he helped me home you see – at the end of the war. He told me he'd once owned a magic shop not far from where I lived –

STAGE MANAGER Are you alright – Mr Nivelli?

NIVELLI Nivelli – yes that was his name. His stage name.

STAGE MANAGER Oh?

NIVELLI I borrowed it you see – because I wanted to – to thank him –

STAGE MANAGER For teaching you your first magic trick?

NIVELLI For everything – but when we reached Frankfurt – he just – and I never saw him again and I never thanked him – you see without him I – I –

Silence.

STAGE MANAGER Mr Nivelli – Ernst – I am just a stage manager – but if I may say – *(Nivelli nods.)* What a career you've had – what joy you've given – to so many. Every time you step onto the stage – you thank this man. I think.

NIVELLI You're very kind. *(The stage manager starts to leave.)* Oh – when I say haven't seen him again – it isn't quite true. I have seen him in a dream.

STAGE MANAGER Oh. *(Looks at his watch.)*

NIVELLI Thank you. Thank you for the tea. *(Exit stage manager. The Great Nivelli looks round. He turns his poster back so that the smile is visible again. He smiles too.)* Yes – yes – I'm sorry.

He goes to his table – there is the same suitcase. He pats it. As a warm up before his show he does a little trick which means putting on the pair of white gloves. He smiles – and thinks –

Music.

NIVELLI *(recorded VO)* In the dream there are bricks everywhere – nothing in order – then these same bricks start to float about to – reassemble themselves into shapes – houses – flats – shops. And then I see him – *(Mr H is standing on the corner of the street – he's holding balloons which float above him.)* And I'm trying to catch his attention but when I try to call out –

NIVELLI *(mouths silently)* Mr H? Mr H?

NIVELLI *(recorded VO)* No sound comes from my lips. Then Mr H is surrounded by people – children mostly – I begin to worry that he won't see me – because he is busy selling the balloons. I try to call again –

NIVELLI   Mr H? Mr H? – Mr Levin.

NIVELLI *(recorded VO)* And he looks up – looks straight at me as if he'd known I was there all along and he smiles that smile only he ever owned.

And then –

Mr H slowly rises from the ground – lifted by the balloons. The Great Mr Nivelli watches as Mr H fades from view.

The end.

SCENE SIX
(with Russian dialogue)

Early morning. It is misty and when Ernst opens his eyes he is not sure what he is seeing. Now he freezes because the shapes become real – two Russian soldiers with rifles raised walking through the mist toward them. One of the soldiers sees that Ernst is staring at him and softly indicates for him to be silent. The other soldier stands behind Mr H who is sleeping.

SOLDIER ONE   Давай вставай, вставай. *(Ernst watches Mr H get to his feet. He looks quite comical as he searches for his hat – knocking things over as he tries to improve his appearance for these unwelcome visitors. Mr H pulls Ernst to him.)* Ты кто? Что ты делаешь?

MR H   Don't shoot – don't shoot.

SOLDIER ONE   Кто ты? Что ты здесь делаешь?

MR H   We don't understand – Hello Hello – um – we don't understand.

SOLDIER ONE   Молчать! Молчать!

MR H   It's alright Ernst – it's –

SOLDIER ONE   Молчать! Молчать! На колени! На колени! Вниз! Вниз!

MR H   I promise you it's alright. Ow.

SOLDIER ONE   Тихо! Что это за хлам? Держи руки вверх! Верх! Что там, в тележке, что в мешках? Оружие, гранаты, ружья? Бум, бум, бум.

MR H   No. No boom, boom. No.

SOLDIER ONE   Открой, открой, давай! Не ты! Ты, парень. Ты! Открывай сейчас!

MR H   Go on Ernst – Go on. Open the suitcase.

SOLDIER ONE   Медленно – медленно. *(Ernst opens the suitcase and steps away as indicated by Soldier Two who then steps forward and peers into the suitcase – then pulls out some clothes – roughly throwing things about.)* Что это?

SOLDIER TWO   Ничего, ерунда.

SOLDIER ONE   Посмотри в тележку.

SOLDIER TWO   Посмотри ты.

SOLDIER ONE   Нет ты посмотри в тележку.

SOLDIER TWO   Нет ты посмотри в тележку.

SOLDIER ONE   Ты.

SOLDIER TWO   ТЫ!

MR H   Wait – me – I look in the cart.

SOLDIER ONE   Стой на месте, стой на месте! Стой на месте. Ты немец?

MR H   Yes. I German. Boy German. You Russian. Trees – wooden.

ERNST   This Russian.

Ernst is holding the leaflet. He holds it out to Soldier Two.

SOLDIER ONE   Осторожно. Осторожно!

SOLDIER TWO   Это лист бумаги. Ты что, боишься листа бумаги?

SOLDIER ONE   Зависит от того, что там написано. Что там написано?

SOLDIER TWO   Я не умею читать, ты же знаешь, что я не умею читать. Почему ты всегда подчеркиваешь это?

MR H   It says – 'The Russians are friends of the German people.'

SOLDIER ONE   Что он сказал?

SOLDIER TWO   Откуда я знаю? Бла, бла, бла.

Soldier Two crumples up the paper and throws it down at Mr H's feet who goes to pick it up.

SOLDIER ONE   Оставь это, назад. Назад!

MR H   Oh I was just – Oh?

To Ernst's surprise where there was a piece of paper is now the bunch of flowers.

SOLDIER ONE   Эй?

SOLDIER TWO   Ха!

Mr H offers them the flowers and performs another trick.

SOLDIER TWO   Ха-ха. Ты это видел?

SOLDIER ONE   Да, видел. Но будь осторожен.

SOLDIER TWO   Не говори мне, что ты боишься букета цветов. Смотри! Опять! (He holds up the gun – to make Mr H do more tricks.) Еще, еще. *(He slowly lowers the gun.)*

Mr H approaches the contents of the suitcase – and from out of nowhere starts to perform tricks by sleight of hand. Soon the soldiers drop their guns and are laughing like children. During this time Mr H relieves Soldier One of a pair of binoculars.

MR H   Ernst – for this one I need your help. Come, come.

They perform another trick.

BOTH SOLDIERS Еще. Еще.

SOLDIER ONE   Ну, ладно, мы пошли.

SOLDIER TWO   Хороший мальчик, у меня дома есть братик, твой ровесник. Хочешь попробовать?

He gives Ernst a drink of vodka. Ernst spits it out. They laugh.

SOLDIER ONE   Это водка. Ну, нам пора идти. До свидания. Удачи вам. Wunderbar.

MR H   Wunderbar. Wunderbar. Goodbye – goodbye – Hey
  for you – friends.

*He gives them some raw rhubarb – which the soldier bites into. The
soldiers have gone. Silence. Mr H sighs deeply – he is shaking.*

ERNST   He'll get diarrhoea.

Scene continues from page 151 as written.

Translation to Russian by Galina Kolosova, February 2013.

Aurora Metro Books

some of our other plays by Charles Way

PLAYS FOR YOUNG PEOPLE
ISBN 978-0-953675-71-5 £9.95

THE CLASSIC FAIRYTALES Retold for the Stage
ISBN 978-0-954233-00-6 £11.50

THE CLASSIC FAIRY TALES 2 Retold for the Stage
ISBN 978-0-955156-67-0 £11.99

THE DUTIFUL DAUGHTER
ISBN 978-0-954691-26-4 £7.99

A SPELL OF COLD WEATHER
ISBN 978-0-954233-08-2 £7.99

MERLIN AND THE CAVE OF DREAMS
ISBN 978-0-955156-60-1 £7.99

some of our other play collections

PLAYS FOR YOUTH THEATRES AND LARGE CASTS by Neil Duffield
ISBN 978-1-906582-06-7 £12.99

THEATRE CENTRE: Plays for Young People selected and introduced by
Rosamunde Hutt
ISBN 978-0-954233-05-1 £12.99

NEW SOUTH AFRICAN PLAYS ed. Charles J. Fourie
ISBN 978-0-954233-01-3 £11.99

BLACK AND ASIAN PLAYS Anthology introduced by Afia Nkrumah
ISBN 978-0-953675-74-6 £12.99

BALKAN PLOTS: New Plays from Central and Eastern Europe ed. Cheryl Robson
ISBN 978-0-953675-73-9 £9.95

www.aurorametro.com